Understanding Your Baby

Understanding Your Child Series

The Tavistock Clinic has an international reputation as a centre of excellence for training, clinical mental health work, research and scholarship. Written by professionals working in the Child and Family and the Adolescent Departments, the guides in this series present balanced and sensitive advice that will help adults to become, or to feel that they are, "good enough" parents. Each book concentrates on a key transition in a child's life from birth to adolescence, looking especially at how parents' emotions and experiences interact with those of their children. The titles in the Understanding Your Child series are essential reading for new and experienced parents, relatives, friends and carers, as well as for the multi-agency professionals who are working to support children and their families.

other titles in the series

Understanding your One-Year-Old
Sarah Gustavus Jones
ISBN 1 84310 241 2

Understanding your Two-Year-Old
Lisa Miller
ISBN 1 84310 288 9

Understanding Your Three-Year-Old
Louise Emanuel
ISBN 1 84310 243 9

Understanding Your Baby

Sophie Boswell

Jessica Kingsley Publishers
London and Philadelphia

First published in the United Kingdom in 2004
by Jessica Kingsley Publishers
116 Pentonville Road
London N1 9JB, England
and
400 Market Street, Suite 400
Philadelphia, PA 19106, USA

www.jkp.com

Copyright © The Tavistock Clinic 2004

Library of Congress Cataloging in Publication Data
Boswell, Sophie, 1969-
Understanding your baby / Sophie Boswell.
    p. cm. — (Understanding your child series)
Includes bibliographical references and index.
ISBN 1-84310-242-0 (alk. paper)
1. Infants. 2. Infants—Development. 3. Mother and infant. I. Title. II. Series.
HQ774.B675 2004
305.232—dc22
                                    2004012451

British Library Cataloguing in Publication Data
A CIP catalogue record for this book is available from the British Library

ISBN 1 84310 242 0

Printed and Bound in Great Britain by
Athenaeum Press, Gateshead, Tyne and Wear

Contents

Foreword

The Tavistock Clinic has an international reputation as a centre of excellence for training, clinical mental health work, research and scholarship. Established in 1920, its history is one of groundbreaking work. The original aim of the Clinic was to offer treatment which could be used as the basis of research into the social prevention and treatment of mental health problems, and to teach these emerging skills to other professionals. Later work turned towards the treatment of trauma, the understanding of conscious and unconscious processes in groups, as well as important and influential work in developmental psychology. Work in perinatal bereavement led to a new understanding within the medical profession of the experience of stillbirth, and of the development of new forms of support for mourning parents and families. The development in the 1950s and 1960s of a systemic model of psychotherapy, focusing on the interaction between children and parents and within families, has grown into the substantial body of theoretical knowledge and therapeutic techniques used in the Tavistock's training and research in family therapy.

The *Understanding Your Child* series has an important place in the history of the Tavistock Clinic. It has been issued in a completely new form three times: in the 1960s, the 1990s, and now, in 2004. Each time the authors, drawing on their clinical background and specialist training, have set out to reflect on the extraordinary story of "ordinary development" as it was observed and experienced at the time. Society changes, of course, and so has this series, as it attempts to make sense of everyday accounts of the ways in which a developing child interacts with his or her parents, carers and the wider world. But within this changing scene there has been something constant, and it is best described as a continuing enthusiasm for a view of development which recognizes the importance of the strong feelings and emotions experienced at each stage of development.

In this engaging first volume, Sophie Boswell sets out to consider how relationships start to form, and how they generally proceed in a thoughtful direction, but she does not shrink from considering rage within relationships, and the intense feelings of frustration that are an ordinary part of the story. The examples that are woven into the text will resonate with those who read this book, who will have experienced similar rage and frustration, and have had to put up with it, too!

Jonathan Bradley
Child Psychotherapist
General Editor of the Understanding Your Child series

Introduction

This book offers insight into the emotional world of a baby, from birth to one year old. Rather than giving direct advice, it provides a different framework for thinking about how a baby feels and behaves, using examples of real situations between parents and their babies.

A central belief behind this book is that a baby cannot be understood in isolation. She is born into a complex relationship with her primary carers, and it is through exploring the intense feelings that a baby both communicates to and provokes in the adults around her that we can build up a richer and more three-dimensional view of what is happening inside her mind. Every baby has an intense emotional life from the day she is born, with her own powerful feelings and unique personality. She both affects and is affected by the feelings and personalities of her parents or closest carers, in ways which they may or may not be aware of. And her parents' own backgrounds, attitudes, mindsets and unconscious feelings will have a major influence on the way she learns about life, and how she relates to the world.

It is important to remember that relationships between parents and babies, like any other, are made up of good and bad qualities. Sometimes we will understand our babies very well, but sometimes we will get things hopelessly wrong. When we do, things will not be broken beyond repair: recovering from difficulties and misunderstandings, for both baby and parents, is an essential part of getting to know and love each other.

Having a baby is a particularly extraordinary and life-changing experience when you encounter it for the first time, and the focus of this book tends to be on first babies. But each new baby will be just as fascinating, bringing her own demands and her own personality, requiring us to readjust and begin the process of discovery right from the beginning each time.

Obviously there are innumerable family situations into which a baby may be born, and I have not been able to do justice to this within the scope of this book. I have assumed that the mother will be the primary caregiver; but the central themes of this book will apply to the father, or to anyone else bringing up a baby. As far as gender is concerned, I have referred to the baby as "he" and "she", alternating between chapters.

1

Pregnancy, Birth and "Bonding"

Perhaps we all enter parenthood with a deep-seated wish to satisfy the needs of another tiny human being, to do everything we can to make her happy. From pregnancy onwards, we strive to provide the perfect environment for our babies, hoping to shield them from the messy and painful things in life. It is easy to feel that if only we can get everything "right" for this new baby – from eating the right things during pregnancy (or feeling tranquil, or playing classical music) through to having a "natural" birth followed by immediate, skin-to-skin contact in the loving arms of two calm and happy parents – then we will be laying the foundations for the most fulfilling of "bonding" experiences, and therefore the best possible start in life.

Of course there is nothing wrong with aiming for this kind of ideal, but we do need to be wary of feeling that any deviation from it means that we have failed our baby or ourselves. "Bonding" takes many forms, and it does not only happen when things are going smoothly. During pregnancy, birth and beyond, we are bound to encounter negative as well as positive feelings, pain as well as pleasure, and distress and anxiety as well as intense happiness. When our baby is born, she too will find herself at the mercy of such extremes of good and bad feelings, as every baby does. And the process of bonding, like the developing of any deep relationship, involves not only enjoying the good things together but also facing painful experiences, and finding ways to recover together.

Pregnancy

A wanted pregnancy can bring pleasure, excitement and pride that are difficult to surpass. Sometimes earlier difficulties can intensify the sense of
achievement when a viable pregnancy finally occurs. For example, Kate
describes how her feelings towards her first baby during pregnancy continued to play a part in their relationship years later:

> I'd already gone through two miscarriages when I became pregnant
> again, and there were concerns about my fertility. I'd more or less
> given up all hope that I would be able to hold on to a pregnancy. But
> when I realized that this one was actually going to stay, I felt so
> grateful to the baby – and after he was born, that feeling stayed. I
> remember feeling it when he was a few days old, when he drank his
> milk, and later when he smiled at me. And in a strange way that grati-
> tude is still there, even now that he's an adult.

Where there have been miscarriages, medical interventions or anxieties about
fertility, parents can feel an overwhelming love and gratitude towards the
unborn baby. In more straightforward pregnancies, too, parents often feel that
the baby has bestowed herself on them like a gift, and this can increase the
warmth and tenderness they feel towards her.

However, in the early weeks of pregnancy, when anxieties about the
baby's well-being are usually at their height, and when a woman can be
feeling half dead with sickness and exhaustion, it is hard to remain consis-
tently starry-eyed about the newcomer. Even women who have looked
forward to pregnancy for years can experience bouts of sadness, depression or
negativity. The needs of a new baby are intense and seem to overshadow
everything else. And while the baby appears to be happy, well nourished and
completely looked after inside the womb, her mother and father might be
feeling much more deprived: tired, unsupported, drained of their own
resources, worried and vulnerable. It can feel as if there is not enough "moth-
ering" to go round.

It is important to bear in mind that such feelings are normal, and may well
feature from time to time, both before and after birth. During pregnancy, and
even more during the early weeks with a new baby, parents are in need of as
much comfort and support as at any other time in their adult lives. At the same
time, they are having to adjust to the fact that they will be occupying themselves for the foreseeable future with the infantile needs of somebody else.
This is a challenging prospect.

Luckily, during most pregnancies there are the "blooming" periods, when the mother feels well again, when parents have the thrill of seeing their baby on ultra-scans flourishing, sucking her thumb, even moving her arms as if in a reassuring wave. There is the pride and excitement in a growing bump – concrete evidence of the baby's survival and growth, restoring the parents' confidence in themselves and their baby. Parents are now more likely to talk to the baby, believe in her as a real person, and enjoy the knowledge that they have created something good.

Life inside the womb

Turning to the baby's experience: a common view is that life in the womb is idyllic – no frustrations, no unmet needs, just peace and tranquillity. Muffled sounds, gentle gurgles from mother's intestines, a heartbeat that is rhythmic and reassuring; dim lighting, food on tap; no hunger, safe and secure boundaries, supported all around by amniotic fluid. No wonder the pregnant woman in her worst state – lugging her extra weight around, unable to sleep, sick, exhausted, hungry – might have pangs of envy or resentment!

Towards the end of pregnancy, we tend to assume that life has become pretty uncomfortable for the baby, as it certainly has for the mother. Whatever we may imagine about life inside, we can be sure of one thing: the unborn baby has become accustomed to her own little world. As far as she is concerned, it *is* the world. So, as she unwittingly approaches the moment of her birth, she is in for a massive shock. Her little world is not only about to be turned upside down, not only changed beyond recognition, but actually lost forever – and replaced by something altogether different.

Labour

So much importance is attached to the way in which a baby enters the world. Perhaps this is because birth is the first and most dramatic separation – mother from baby and baby from mother. Even though most parents will be counting the days and weeks until they finally meet their baby, anticipating this first moment of separation can stir up all sorts of anxieties. Attitudes towards childbirth – pain relief or not, medical versus natural, home versus hospital – can throw up a whole array of different fantasies about what the separating of mother and baby will be like.

Some parents project their fears onto the medical profession, seeing doctors as a hostile, interfering presence threatening the fulfilling experience they long for. Others see the dangers more inside their own bodies: the physical pain and medical risks fill them with dread, and they are glad to place themselves in the hands of experienced professionals to get them safely through. Many parents find it reassuring to try to claim back some control for themselves through detailed birth plans and childbirth classes.

However much we prepare for childbirth, finding ourselves in completely unknown and unpredictable territory is something we will have to deal with, both during the birth and immediately afterwards with our newborn baby. The experience of childbirth challenges many of our assumptions about ourselves, at the deepest level. There is no way of predicting how we will feel or react. We just have to try to accept that both baby and parents are entering one of the most demanding transitions of their lives. We can only try to manage what is thrown at us, appreciating that we, like the baby, may need plenty of time and space to find our bearings afterwards.

The moment of birth

The parents' experience

The first few moments of a new baby's life stir up powerful, primitive feelings. Susan, a first-time mother, remembers her son's birth.

> I'd ended up having a caesarean and had to wait while they stitched me up, cleaned him and checked him out. But I was aching to hold him, and very tearful – I don't know if it was relief, or just feeling I couldn't wait another second. I just wanted him in my arms. I kept thinking, this is my baby, not yours! When I finally held him we were in the recovery room, and the doctors were laughing because he was sucking away on his hand, ready for a feed. It was so wonderful to finally hold him, I was shaking all over, and I couldn't stop crying. I didn't feel like myself any more.

Many parents feel that during labour they "lose" themselves. Everything else seems to stop, and their ordinary experiences – time passing, the world carrying on around them – suddenly seem insignificant next to the extraordinary experience they are having. Parents often feel shaken and shocked, not sure where they are any more, perhaps even not sure *who* they are. It is in this state that they meet their baby for the first time – another person who has lost herself, only in her case she really doesn't know who she is, or where she is, or what on earth has just happened. It is a moment unlike any other. Perhaps it is in this state, when we are less sure of ourselves than at any other time, that we are closest to understanding something of what our baby might be experiencing. And it is out of these beginnings, out of all this chaos and lost identities that a mother, father and baby begin finding themselves and each other in a completely new way.

The baby's experience

It is tempting to imagine that during birth a baby is able to switch off, so that she doesn't have to be conscious of the pulling, or the sucking, or the wrenching sensations, possibly the pain of being squeezed and compressed, or perhaps the terror as she loses the world she knows, as everything suddenly changes, and she finds herself after an eternity of time in a world that is completely new.

We might feel out of control during labour, but it is hard to imagine how out of control the baby must feel. From the warm, fluid environment of the womb, she is now in an enormous space with no boundaries to support her, a cold, airy space, with new colours, new sights that are constantly changing – let alone the bodily sensations she has never known: the newness of breath coming in and out of her lungs, the sounds of unmuffled voices, perhaps of her own crying, the shock of gravity, and of hunger. Most babies are able to show their shock straight away, crying out urgently as soon as they have breath in their lungs. Others take more time in expressing any response, perhaps retreating to a state of confusion or sleepiness, not yet ready to take in the newness of it all.

Offering comfort

Most adults feel intuitively that a newborn baby will find comfort in things that are as close to being familiar as possible. We try to reproduce as much of the internal uterine situation as we can, wrapping her up securely, keeping her warm, allowing her to hear the voices of her mother and father which she will recognize from the womb. And, of course, offering food as soon as she needs it.

Mentally, too, the newborn needs to have her feelings wrapped up and held on to, as she will fear that all the chaos inside her might be unmanageable. This is done instinctively by a mother who is still closely connected and in tune with her baby, perhaps without being conscious of it, and responds on a deep level to her baby's distress. Even if a mother feels out of her depth, unsure about what to do, her absorption in her baby and intense feelings about her are part of what the baby needs, to feel less alone and unintegrated.

"Bonding"

Even at this stage, many parents are concerned that there is a "right" and a "wrong" way to do things, and that the innocent baby may be damaged if her parents get things "wrong". Perhaps early bonding is the most emotive of these areas. A great deal has been said about the importance of bonding with your baby immediately after birth, and parents can begin to feel as if their child's future happiness depends on these first few hours of life.

Some parents become frightened that certain interventions during labour will have interfered with the all-important first hours with their babies: too many drugs during labour leading to a comatose baby or one who won't be able to breastfeed; a traumatic experience resulting in post-natal depression; an emergency caesarean, particularly with a general anaesthetic, inflicting early separation trauma on the baby, spoiling the bonding processes between mother and child. Sometimes a mother or father is shocked and worried to discover their immediate feelings on greeting their child are not at all what they had expected. Feelings such as hostility, fear or even indifference can leave them frightened that their relationship with the baby will be damaged forever.

But we all "bond" with our babies in different ways, and to our own and our babies' timescales. Of course, some first few hours can be more pleasurable than others, leaving parents more relaxed and ready to enjoy their babies. But it would be foolish to suggest that there is an absolute correlation between a positive labour and successful bonding. Whatever kind of labour we have, things can feel difficult or unreal in the first few hours after our babies are born. We might feel weepy, exhausted and bewildered; our babies might cry all night, or appear sleepy and unresponsive. It is not uncommon that the experience of birth is a let-down, and some parents do feel sad, angry or regretful if things did not go according to plan.

Fathers will have their own set of issues to come to terms with too. There is a tendency to underestimate or belittle the needs of a father around child-birth. It is true, the father escapes physical pain – but remaining supportive and rock-like is not easy in what are often fraught and emotional situations. A father may be left feeling shell-shocked in his own right, especially if he has had to witness his partner in severe pain, possibly also bearing considerable anxiety about her safety and that of his unborn baby.

Recovery

All of this can be difficult and upsetting for anybody involved, and may well take time to heal. Both parents can find it a relief to find a sympathetic relative or friend with whom to talk through their experiences, reliving the stress or the pain they have been through. For some parents a difficult birth can exacerbate more deep-seated issues in their lives which might rise to the surface, making them feel much more vulnerable. But it is important to remember that in these early hours nothing gets set in stone. It is possible to recover from difficult beginnings, and to help our babies to recover as well. This can be a fundamental part of "bonding".

After a particularly gruelling, 28-hour labour which ended in an emergency caesarean under general anaesthetic, a midwife popped in to see how two first-time parents were coping. She found the mother, exhausted by her marathon labour, lying in bed in a deep sleep. Her husband, who had been supporting her throughout the birth, was sitting on the chair next to her bed, holding his new daughter in his arms – both of them were fast asleep, too. This was the way this particular family began the process of "bonding" – sharing a well-earned rest, after what they had all been through.

Birth is the first of many intense emotional experiences that we will go through with our babies, and there is something moving about the way in which both parents and babies can recover from even the most fraught of beginnings. Whether we have a wonderful home birth or an extended, painful labour, a traumatic experience of emergency intervention, an elective caesarean, or a quick and easy delivery, we have just as much potential to be good parents, to bond with our babies, to love them and look after them.

The baby's initial responses to life

Babies are born with distinctive personalities. Some seem to be born hungry for life and all it has to offer, ready to suck as soon as they get the chance. Others appear to be more wary, perhaps not so sure life outside the womb is going to be very easy to digest. Some fight for what they need, but become panicky if the food doesn't come straight away, terrified that such urgent needs might not be met. Others are more easily comforted, and seem able to hold on for a little bit longer before they get into a hopeless state. Often, babies who are born early seem to go at a slower pace, not quite ready to launch themselves into the world, perhaps spending most of their time asleep in the first few days. They seem to need more protection from the bombardment of new sensations which they have suddenly encountered.

First few days: being beginners

Having finally met her, most new parents can't take their eyes off their new baby and are totally absorbed, finding every detail utterly miraculous and wonderful. A newborn baby is endlessly fascinating, and in many ways still unknown. As we come to terms with the discoveries that are coming thick and fast, friends and relatives can offer invaluable support, advice and admiration. The excitement and the heightened status of new parents can wrap them in a bubble of unreality and euphoria.

Sometimes new parents feel under pressure to show the world that they are already competent, happy, "natural" – even if deep down they are feeling raw, emotional and out of their depth. Some first-time mothers are less at ease in hospital, feeling intimidated or undermined by the impersonal environment of a hospital ward, and this can intensify their preoccupation with living up to expectations – although usually this will come from within themselves as much as from the outside world. Others might feel much more supported in hospital and scared at the thought of going home, where they might not know how to cope without all the advice and expertise of the hospital staff.

Childbirth and the early days are often much more "messy" than parents could have imagined, both physically and emotionally. Both parents are having to come to terms with having their lives changed completely and, combined with exhaustion, this inevitably throws up new tensions and frictions between them. It seems inevitable that at some stage most parents will be feeling wobbly and scared, in between the more euphoric moments. This is far from being a sign of failure. In fact, as long as we don't lose our grip altogether, we could find that we are better able to respond to our babies' emotional state if we are more in touch with our own, with all the rawness this entails.

Many women can find themselves trying to live up to an image of effortless motherhood. This is a losing battle. It is much easier to find our way when we allow ourselves to be beginners, and let our baby be a beginner too, leaning on other people when we need to, accepting the fact that we might feel miserable sometimes, and being patient with our own and our baby's imperfections. Ideals of motherhood can also get in the way of the primary task, which is getting to know the new baby, remaining as open as we can to what she is communicating, and being as true to ourselves as we possibly can along the way.

First feeds

There is something reassuring, almost miraculous, about seeing a newborn baby take in milk, whether from breast or bottle. But while the hungry baby can latch on to breast or bottle immediately, showing her mother that she knows exactly what to do, the more withdrawn or sleepy baby might need hours of encouragement and coaxing. For new parents, who may well be exhausted and drained after labour, the challenge of feeding an uninterested baby can be extremely stressful. The sense of your baby being on the edge of life and death is at its height during childbirth, but the feelings connected to feeding a newborn baby can be just as extreme.

Bottle or breast?

Most mothers have strong preconceptions about how they will feed their babies and what feeding will be like. But just as most of us find that the best-laid birth plan can become redundant when we encounter the reality of labour, so the issues that can arise around feeding are much more emotional and beyond our control than we could have envisaged.

Sometimes a mother is amazed when her baby is born knowing what to do, taking control of the situation by latching on and sucking vigorously from day one. This can give a wonderful boost to her self-esteem and confidence in breastfeeding. But some women who envisaged happily breastfeeding their babies are shocked to find that things are much more complicated, often for reasons no one can fully explain. In some situations – where there are inverted or very painful nipples, a baby who doesn't latch on, or failure to gain weight – it can take a huge amount of perseverance and stamina to keep going until breastfeeding becomes something enjoyable rather than stressful. For some women this can be terribly disappointing, soul-destroying and threatening to their belief in themselves as "good" mothers.

Other women begin breastfeeding only to find themselves plagued by worries about their milk supply: will the milk really be good enough? Will there ever be enough to satisfy a seemingly insatiable baby? Even when a baby is putting on weight and all seems to be well, these anxieties can sometimes undermine the feeding relationship.

Breastfeeding is a very emotive issue, and like childbirth, provokes strong and passionate feelings about what is and isn't "natural". This can pile on the pressure when a mother and baby are struggling to find out what is best for them. A mother who would really prefer to bottle feed her baby might keep on breastfeeding for fear of failing her baby, even if this goes against her instincts; by the same token, another might turn to bottle feeding because she cannot get breastfeeding right the first few times, and won't allow herself the chance to work at it until it becomes more comfortable. It would certainly be easier to listen to ourselves and our babies, discovering what works best for us, if we didn't feel so laden down with value judgements.

We should never forget that babies are part of the feeding relationship too, and have their part to play in the decision. Those who take to breastfeeding with gusto might be able to convince a doubtful mother that it is worth persevering; while babies who seem unsure, or who show little interest in taking to the breast, might persuade a wavering mother to give up. The close-knit relationship between mother and baby means that it is never quite clear whose feelings are whose, or where certain anxieties or preferences begin and end.

Breastfeeding can provide some of the most intimate and precious moments between a mother and her baby, offering a particular form of closeness and pleasure together. However, if breastfeeding doesn't work out, this doesn't mean that the mother and baby will be deprived of closeness and intimacy. Feeding a baby with a bottle can be a wonderful experience in its own right, and of course, every mother and baby find countless different ways to communicate love and warmth. If attempts at breastfeeding have been anxious or unsatisfying for both parties, it can make the world of difference when feeds become enjoyable for the first time. From the baby's perspective, the most important thing is that feeding should be something enjoyable, given and received with pleasure. A more relaxed mother is better able to reassure her baby, however she ends up feeding her, than one who is stressed or uncomfortable with what she is doing.

Getting to know your baby

While you can sit and stare at your baby for hours, admiring her perfections, any signs of irregularity can suddenly loom large, bringing back deep-seated fears about whether this tiny creature can really survive. It is difficult to judge what is normal, or when outside help is needed – perhaps because a baby can become terrified or distraught when things are feeling wrong inside her, physically or emotionally, and we are bound to be caught up in the force of her feelings.

Louise describes her first moment of this kind of doubt, when her daughter was three days old.

> Annie had been crying painfully, as if something was really hurting her – and then we noticed that her poo was really runny, and I immediately decided that she must be dangerously ill. I panicked. I couldn't think straight, my heart was pounding and I was sure she was going to die. I hadn't realized how absolutely terrifying it could be, even the smallest possibility that something could be wrong with her.

Most parents have moments like this, when the survival of their baby suddenly seems terrifyingly fragile, and they are overcome by the depth of their need for this baby to be all right. Even a baby who has been asleep for longer than usual can send parents rushing to her bedside to check that she is still breathing. Of course, there are times when these fears actually do become real, and a baby is seriously ill. But when, as in most cases, the symptoms we have become so preoccupied by turn out to be perfectly harmless, we can usually recover our balance quite quickly, and go back to seeing our baby as strong and full of potential, with a reassuring drive towards life and growth. These sudden lurches of mood are very typical of early life with a baby, illustrating the rawness and extremes of emotion which a newborn baby brings with her.

Helpful advice, and feeling judged

No other relationship in our lives involves so many opinions about the right and wrong way of conducting ourselves. Perhaps because there is something so vulnerable and helpless about babies, people feel deeply about "doing the right thing" by them. Seeing an upset or panicky baby is very hard to bear without coming up with the "solution". It is hard to accept the fact that all parents, however competent, will get it wrong sometimes and that babies are capable of putting up with a fair amount of misunderstandings and mistakes that are bound to occur, especially at the very beginning. It takes time to get to know what our baby needs and what we can and can't provide for her.

There are times when we desperately need help, support and advice from other adults. For example, it is surprisingly hard as a first-time parent to spot when your baby is crying from sheer exhaustion, rather than insatiable hunger or existential misery. Quite often it will take a third party to suggest this simple but elusive explanation; this can offer us a way out of the inevitable spirals of frustration which a tired baby can bring – even if passing this insight on to the baby may prove more difficult!

There are also times when we need some space to work things out for ourselves, and to learn from our own mistakes. Particularly during the first few days with a new baby, it is important that we take time to work out where we are with our babies, and get used to ourselves as parents, without feeling too loaded down by all the knowledge and advice being heaped on us by friends and relatives. We are still adjusting to the fact that having a baby, bonding and becoming a family do not lend themselves to smoothness or perfection: we are living with our own humanness, and that of our baby. It helps if we are not too critical or demanding of ourselves, but accept that we and our baby first and foremost need time together to begin the long, complex and fascinating task of getting to know each other.

2

The First Six Weeks

Highs and lows

For most parents – and no doubt for most babies, too – the first six weeks are the hardest. The intense attention and drama of labour and post-natal care are gone, and suddenly being left alone with a new baby is a daunting experience. Many mothers describe their terror when the midwife announces that she won't be visiting again. It is particularly hard that the time when babies are most frightened and vulnerable, the first few weeks of their lives, is the time when new parents are most vulnerable too, uncertain about whether they will be good enough parents, and whether their baby will really survive and flourish. The learning curve is dramatically steep for everyone involved.

There is something miraculous about a new baby's capacity to survive, even though it is also the most ordinary thing in the world. Andrew describes his feelings in the first few days of his daughter's life.

> She was just so tiny and so precious. When she was asleep I couldn't take my eyes off her, thinking, "It can't really be true, we can't really be allowed to keep her forever." Half the time I felt like I was in another world, just floating.

A new baby fills your mind and becomes your whole world. When things are going well, the pride, pleasure and excitement are indescribable. When things are difficult, it can feel like the end of the world. Andrew's partner, Julie, saw the early weeks as like being at sea.

> One minute I was riding the waves, bursting with pride: I had the best baby in the world, and I'd always make her happy. The next thing I

knew everything was upside down. She would suddenly be crying and miserable, and I didn't know why, and often I'd become miserable too, in tears myself, thinking "What am I doing wrong?" And then it was more like trying not to drown.

During these early weeks passions run high for babies and for those caring for them, and all these strong emotions can leave parents reeling. It is worth remembering that for most parents this period is exceptionally hard work, and that the ups and downs usually become less extreme as time passes and the baby becomes more relaxed and easier to understand.

Chaos versus routine

One of the most demanding aspects of a newborn baby is the way in which his life has no structure or predictability. It is very common for a newborn baby to spend most of one day sleeping, most of the next feeding, then the following night alert or hungry, with no apparent rhythm or routine. This can be utterly bewildering and disconcerting for a new mother or father, who can't help but expect some sort of logic or consistency to their baby's sleeping and feeding patterns, and assume they must be doing something wrong. But our ordered world must seem like chaos to the newborn. New sensations such as hunger and gravity; different temperatures and textures on his skin; new smells, new atmospheres, and a whole array of new sights and sounds replace the only rhythm and routine he has ever known, inside the womb.

It takes time, and for some babies more time than others, before they can gradually get used to their new life and adapt to the expectations we put on them. Some parents find the lack of routine relatively manageable; for others the need to impose some kind of order is stronger, or comes into play earlier. It is important to remember that we are all going to need help, and that this can take different forms. Some parents rely on books or magazines to provide a framework for coping with the chaos. A supportive partner can be invaluable in making the intensity less threatening, by sharing the experience, the childcare and the anxieties that accompany it. Many mothers need somebody to talk to, a friend, health visitor, parent or post-natal group, to get things into perspective so that they can face the apparently endless demands of their babies feeling more supported.

At a few days old Cathy's first baby, Kirsty, was waking up every two hours in the night, crying bitterly and wanting to be fed. In the daytime, Cathy found herself carrying Kirsty around the house in a sling, as she settled only when she was being held. By the end of Kirsty's first two weeks, Cathy was exhausted and desperate.

> I felt my entire life had been taken away from me. I couldn't enjoy meals any more because I always seemed to be feeding Kirsty, or had her clamped to my chest, I couldn't even go to the toilet without her. My friends kept saying I must be so happy, and I kept saying "Oh, yes!" But deep down, I wasn't. I wouldn't have admitted it, but this wonderful thing, that I'd been looking forward to so much, was feeling more like a nightmare.

Cathy eventually turned to a book offering advice about getting babies into a routine.

> At first I thought it was so cruel. I hated the idea of letting Kirsty cry for even a few minutes. I was terrified that nothing would change. But I just kept working on it, and I kept going back to the book. It never went exactly like it said, but after a while I realized that when she was upset I could say to her, "No, Kirsty, you're tired, go to sleep properly now", and put her down knowing she'd go off to sleep eventually. I was surprised how often it worked, but even when it didn't I felt calmer about things. It felt like Kirsty wasn't ruling my life any more, and I think it gave me back some confidence. I started to think, "Maybe I can do this!"

The different needs of mothers are just as important as those of their babies. For Cathy, the relentless needs of a demanding baby simply felt too much, and for her own sake she needed to claim back some control. Perhaps the book Cathy found so helpful served almost like a motherly presence, offering her some advice and perspective which at that time she had lost. With this support, she felt less frightened by her baby's distress, and less enslaved to her every demand. This probably helped Kirsty, too, as it meant her mother was feeling less distraught and more able to rally her own resources. Babies are well known for picking up on their mother or father's states of mind – something that will be discussed later in this chapter.

If, like Cathy, we do find it helpful to guide our babies towards a more routined pattern of behaviour during the first few weeks, it is vital that we remain open to what our babies are communicating to us, and need us to understand. They *will* be feeling bewildered and lost much of the time, and life will sometimes feel chaotic, frightening and without boundaries. If we can take this on board, while at the same time discovering ways to alleviate our own fears of slipping into chaos, we are in a better position to help our babies feel safer and less out of control, too.

Guidelines or routines don't work for everybody. Some parents might prefer going with the flow, some might dislike being told what to do, and naturally some find that their babies just won't behave like they do in the books. If we do follow a less structured course, allowing our babies to find their own rhythm in their own time, putting up with the sleepless nights and blurry days, we must be careful not to lose sight of our own need for stability and time to ourselves as adults. Without keeping hold of some of our own boundaries and our own perspectives, we can end up feeling enslaved to our babies, exhausted and beleaguered. If this happens it is not just we who might become overwhelmed. Often a baby will respond by becoming more frightened, too.

But of course, during these difficult early weeks there are also moments of intense pleasure. Seeing your baby putting on weight, as skinny limbs become soft and round; the warmth of a well-fed baby, sleeping peacefully on your chest; early glimpses of smiles, all building up a sense of progress and growing enjoyment. Perhaps most reassuring of all, there are the times when you *do* get it right, realizing with exhilaration that your presence and your comfort are exactly what your baby needs. There are more and more lights at the end of the tunnel.

Responding to a baby's distress

Most parents feel that they should be able to shield their newborn baby from the ordinary strains and miseries that are part of being human. We desperately want our offspring to be happy, and it can be a shock in the first few weeks to recognize that our baby, like every other, however loved and cherished, will have his share of unhappiness. Knowing that babies cry is one thing; witnessing the raw and passionate emotions of your own newborn child is quite another.

Babies in their first few weeks seem to be desperately searching for something that might feel like "home" – to find their way in a foreign environment full of new sensations and feelings. A baby has no means for thinking about any of this; life is just a mass of chaotic impressions and feelings. After all, such small babies cannot predict what might happen next, nor can they be sure of holding on to memories of what has just happened. This makes them incredibly vulnerable to sudden shocks. They can appear blissfully contented, perhaps when they are safe in their mother or father's arms, enjoying their milk, warm and safe, feeling that the world is a wonderful place. But they can suddenly look as if the whole world is falling apart, perhaps when the food is not coming, and they have no way of knowing that it will ever come again. They cry out, trying to rid themselves of these nasty feelings. Their faces turn red and contorted in misery; hands and legs flail about as if in a rage against the world; or they tip over into those painful, urgent sobs which can be so heartbreaking. And when they seem to have descended into utter misery, we can feel completely helpless to take their sufferings away.

Often parents, particularly mothers, feel personally responsible for any signs of distress, and guilty if they cannot remove whatever is causing it straight away. Some parents find the cry of their newborn baby almost physically painful. It is hard to tolerate our baby's cries without being able to comfort him, and we can end up feeling angry and despairing ourselves. A baby will often look at us with panic when things go wrong, as if it is all our fault. This is probably an inevitable part of becoming a parent, and if our baby's crying couldn't provoke such concern in us he wouldn't get the high level of attention and concern he needs. How well we cope with this has a lot to do with how tightly we can hold on to a calmer perspective, while we are steeped in the infantile distress a new baby brings.

A mother and baby panic together

James, at two weeks old, became inconsolable when his mother, Anna, gave him his first bath at home.

> The midwife told me to bath him before a feed, so he wouldn't be sick. But when I put him down to get him ready he seemed to panic. I'm sure he was expecting a feed, and when it didn't come, his world fell apart.

As James got more distressed, Anna began to feel panicky herself.

> When I took his clothes off he looked at me with his eyes full of terror, as if I'd turned into a witch. It made me feel terrible. His little arms kept on jerking out, as if he was falling off a cliff and trying to grasp hold of something. He looked so desperate, but nothing I did seemed to help. He kept forcing his fingers into his mouth and sucking hard, as if he had to believe that milk would come out. When

I actually put him into the bath he just lost it completely, his whole body shaking with sobs. I found it difficult to hold him, my hands were shaking and I just wanted to cry. In the end, when he was finally out and dry, he calmed down and I fed him. He stretched out and then went to sleep in my arms. Only then I could breathe again.

This is an example of how a mother can become so caught up in feeling with her baby in a moment of distress that she loses her foothold, finding it difficult to help him get through an ordinary but stressful situation. What started as the baby's fear became the mother's fear too, and with so much guilt and anxiety to contend with, no wonder she struggled to handle him in a calm or reassuring way.

James seems to be experiencing a state of disintegration – something which a newborn baby is particularly susceptible to, with his fragile sense of self. When the milk he wants fails to appear, his equilibrium is profoundly shaken; he then becomes more and more anxious as his mother removes his clothes, until he feels he has lost his grip on both his body and his mind, fearing that he is falling apart. He shows this physically in his desperate jerking around, as if his body is under attack, and he doesn't know whether he can survive such a threat. Emotionally he is in much the same state, having lost his connection to anything good in himself or in his mother. He searches in a panic for something to cling to, a nipple or teat, which might help him feel whole again, or restore his sense of being safely inside his own skin.

When a baby's feelings are so raw, we do need to take these feelings on board for him, conveying to him that we know what he is going through, even feeling some of it with him. But it is important that we hold on to our adult perspective, too. This can be very difficult, and most parents find themselves drawn right in to their children's distress from time to time. For another mother – or the same mother in a more robust mood – this baby's distress might have provoked sympathy and sorrow, rather than such strong fellow-feeling and anxiety. It is impossible to get it right every time. As Anna discovered, the process of making up, finding each other again and repairing any damage done, is a vital part of getting to know one another and gaining more faith that such states can be recovered from. After this disastrous attempt, Anna took to having James in the bath with her, where they both felt calmer and bath times became enjoyable.

How the parents' moods affect the baby

From the earliest days, babies are highly sensitive to their parents' states of mind. They can be comforted by a calm presence, or become more agitated when held by somebody in an anxious state. This knowledge can provide a helpful clue as to what might be bothering an unhappy baby. Most of us have got to our wits' end with a crying, fractious baby, who immediately becomes calm and contented the minute somebody else takes him. This might seem like an indictment of our parenting abilities. But sometimes, when it has all got too much, any mother and baby can end up getting under one another's skin and simply need a bit of time away from each other. Over time mother, father, grandparents and baby will gradually get to know one another's personalities better, and discover ways to overcome the difficulties that are bound to come up between them from time to time.

However, parents already feel responsible for any sign of unhappiness in their babies, and the thought that we might be contributing to it can lead to spirals of guilt. Blaming ourselves does not achieve very much: it is likely to increase our anxiety, making things more difficult for everyone concerned. There is a happy medium between ignoring our influence on our baby's mood, and becoming convinced that every flicker of emotion in our baby must be due to us. We have to try to weather each storm, remembering that we are reacting to our babies' moods just as much as they are reacting to ours. It goes without saying that all parents will have limitations and problems – a baby wouldn't have much joy from a "perfect" parent. This relationship, like every other, is enriched by its ups and downs.

How the baby's moods affect the parents

Babies are powerful little creatures with strong personalities, and their own intense emotional states strongly affect the feelings and moods of those caring for them.

The extreme states of mind that the baby is having to cope with are not far away from the kinds of feelings a mother can be facing alongside her baby. As first-time parents we can often feel that we have been plunged into an alien and rather terrifying world, where we have to learn our way around with amazing speed in order not to feel lost. Babies bring their turbulence with them and the urgency of their terror can be so powerful that we can feel that we have lost our bearings completely.

Strong childlike feelings about our own parents can make a surprise reappearance when we become parents ourselves. We might feel a new solidarity with our parents, realizing what they went through when we were babies. We might find ourselves highly critical of them, vowing to do things differently. Some parents feel that their babies are getting a better experience of parenting than they themselves did, which can cause both comfort and sadness. Many new mothers describe feelings of homesickness, a longing for their own childhood mothers or fathers, or sudden loneliness, which make them feel particularly raw and vulnerable. Fathers, too, can be surprised when issues from their own childhood can suddenly press down on them, causing anxiety or a surge of strong emotion.

Matt, on becoming a father for the first time, found himself feeling churned up in a way he hadn't expected.

> I'd never known my own father, and suddenly here I was being a father to Thomas. One day when he was about two weeks old I was washing up and suddenly I was in floods of tears. I never remember missing my father when I was growing up, but I suddenly felt I was missing him now.

Matt's new baby had brought him in touch with feelings that he hadn't had since he was a very young child.

It can be difficult to deal with experiences like this while simultaneously coping with the huge emotional demands of a new baby. But such states are not only an inevitable part of what we are going through – they can also make us particularly well placed to empathize with our babies and remain in touch with their raw emotions and neediness. All of this will make us more able to offer them the comfort and reassurance they need.

Coping with dependency

New parents are often gripped by a fear that their baby's crying, sleeplessness, colic or absolute dependency are never going to stop. Over time, they discover that things do get easier, as the baby becomes more resilient and better at tolerating frustration. But how does a newborn baby know – and how do first-time parents really know – that each phase will not last forever? There is a particular anxiety about letting small babies become too dependent on a certain thing – sleeping in the parents' bed, feeding on demand, dummies, being picked up each time they cry, or being allowed to fall asleep at breast or bottle – in case such things get set in stone. New parents are often warned they are making "a rod for their own back" by letting such indulgences go unchecked, or that they are "spoiling" the baby and will regret it later.

Maria was breastfeeding her two-week-old baby, Ella.

Everyone kept saying, "feed her on demand", but I couldn't believe they really meant it, or at least, they hadn't met Ella! Each feed lasted almost an hour, so I could never get anything done, and every time I broke off she seemed to get upset and want more. I couldn't believe she was hungry all the time, so I tried everything I could think of to hold her off, walking around the house, dancing her up and down. In the end it started to annoy me, and sometimes I'd turn the music up to try and drown out the incessant crying.

Maria, like many mothers, seemed to become frightened by the seemingly endless needs of her new baby, and when the distress felt unbearable she found herself switching off. Maria talked to her midwife, who offered a different response.

She was a kind woman, and I remember how gently she spoke about Ella. She said Ella was very tiny and frightened, and that it was normal for her to want to be at the breast much of the time, and I shouldn't try and stop her. It was a bit of a surprise, in a way, because to me Ella hadn't seemed tiny at all. She seemed huge, especially when she was screaming her head off. When I looked at her through the midwife's eyes, I thought, "My God, she's much more scared than I am!" After that I stopped thinking I was giving in to her too much, and I let her have the breast more often. It was quite a relief. She seemed a lot happier, and things sort of slotted into place after that.

Feeling that her daughter's needs were huge and insatiable, Maria seemed to lose hope that she could do anything to alleviate them. Perhaps this is why she found herself cutting herself off from Ella's vulnerability. This kind of anxiety often stems from a belief that a new baby's needs are endless, and will never change. In fact this is not true. The baby might believe it, and feel it so strongly that he can even convince us at times. But we can help him to learn otherwise, if we work hard at keeping our perspective.

Like Maria, if we try to imagine what it is like to be a week or two old, utterly lost and bewildered, it is hard to see how receiving comfort could bring anything but good. If a newborn baby, like Ella, gets most reassurance from sucking on the breast, whether for comfort or milk, letting him do this as much as we reasonably can helps him to feel that the world is a safe enough place, that comfort generally comes when you need it. With enough of these good experiences, he will begin to feel stronger inside and more comfortable in his own skin, more able to deal with the horrible feelings that suddenly attack him when the world goes bad on him again.

Although it can be difficult to stay in touch with such neediness, it is important that we keep trying, and not lose sight of how tiny and vulnerable a baby is. Through responding to the urgency of his needs when he is most helpless, we are paving the way for him to learn gradually to enjoy a bit more variety in his life, and to cope with small doses of frustration. Later, when he is more resourceful in himself, we can begin thinking about weaning him away from any sources of comfort that he might no longer need.

In Maria's case, she found that after a few weeks of demand feeding, Ella stopped getting so worked up between feeds, and began to find other sources of comfort and pleasure in her life: the fear of endless feeding became a thing of the past.

Coping with frustration

Obviously, some babies can cope with a bit more frustration earlier than others, just as parents vary as to how much distress or discomfort they can bear to witness. As we saw earlier, judging when a baby is ready to have some order imposed on his feeds, sleep further away from his parents, cry a little before going off to sleep, and so on, is not something we can know automatically. For each parent and child it has to be a matter of trial and error, part of the process of getting to know our baby and what he can and cannot manage. Gradually we will face the task of gently helping him to move on to the next stage. During the very early weeks, most babies can deal with frustration only in very small doses, and they need to feel that we can tolerate their helplessness; we also need to keep in mind – for their sake and for ours – that it won't last forever.

Love

Some parents feel love for their babies straight away. Others are shocked that they don't feel loving at all, even strangely detached. It is common to feel deflated and disappointed, just as it is to be bursting with pride. Danny, a second-time father, described feeling a surge of tenderness and protectiveness towards his little daughter, but not what he would call love.

> I knew that I felt strongly for her, and my whole world seemed to be taken over with every little detail about her. But how could I love someone I didn't even know yet?

At this stage of a baby's life, parents often feel that their tiny offspring are not able to "give much back". It is often weeks of relentless parenting, devotion, self-sacrifice and attentiveness before we are given our first real smile. What can be most rewarding, though, is the sense that we are providing the most essential things for our babies, and that they are beginning to feel more at home in the world.

It can seem to parents that a baby's view of the world is stark. He can look at us as if we were the best thing in the whole world one moment, and the next as if we had turned into monsters. At this stage he doesn't know the difference between things that happen in his mind and things that happen in his body. One example of this is colic, or "gripe". As adults, we know that a gripping pain in the stomach can signify anxiety or fear, as well as physical illness. For a young baby, these are one and the same thing. Tummy ache is painful and causes anxiety, just as anxiety is painful and causes tummy ache – there is absolutely no way for him to distinguish one from the other. When he is in pain he needs comfort both physically and emotionally.

In the same way, a baby seems unable to identify where he ends and another person begins. "Mother" or "father" might mean a collection of particular smells, sounds or sensations. No wonder a baby of a few weeks old can look at us in apparent horror, believing it is our fault that his world has suddenly fallen apart, when overcome by hunger, pain or frustration. When the whole world has turned bad, he has no capacity to remember that we are nice sometimes, or imagine that we will ever be nice again. Similarly, at moments of utter contentment, gazing at his mother during a satisfying feed, or half asleep on his father's shoulder, being rocked tenderly, he looks as if the world has become a blissful and altogether wonderful place. We have turned into figures that are completely good, all former crimes blotted out.

Babies have passionate feelings, but wouldn't be able to feel "love" or "hate" as we understand them. They appear to experience a more general, all-encompassing feeling of "loveliness" when things are good or "hatefulness" when they are bad. Their primary business at this stage is still learning to survive what life has thrown at them, and there will be more room for complex human emotions later on. Perhaps for their carers, too, the new relationship can feel like a roller-coaster ride between extreme emotions. Only later, as babies begin to open out and explore the world of other people, and are able to see us as real people, do we find ourselves relating to them in a more three-dimensional way.

Feeling low, and negative thoughts about the baby

I have said a bit about the vulnerability of new mothers, and the tendency to feel overwhelmed and raw, particularly in the first few weeks. Jo, after the birth of her first baby, described a huge sense of loss, almost as if she was grieving for something.

> I didn't know what it was I had lost – perhaps it was just having the baby inside me. But I couldn't stop crying, and I felt lonely and miserable for quite a while. I think I would have given anything to be a baby again myself, not having to think about anyone else, just constantly being cuddled and looked after.

Probably every mother has periods of feeling low or depressed after the birth of her first baby. Usually these states alternate with excitement and happiness, but sometimes they are more prolonged and can feel worrying. Many mothers are frightened of post-natal depression, putting themselves under pressure to "be happy" all the time. However, mood swings are normal during this period, and not many mothers escape without days of feeling absolutely miserable, lonely or depressed. This in itself will not damage your baby. It is bound to make life more difficult for both mother and baby for a while, but being emotional and a bit raw does not amount to being clinically depressed. It is not surprising that mothers should find themselves encountering a very full and intense range of feelings; they have their own infantile feelings to deal with, their altered lifestyle and identity. Most of all, they are being asked to empathize with the hugely varying and extreme states of mind which their babies are going through, and to provide comfort and understanding on call.

Not surprisingly, negative feelings about the baby can also emerge. For Hanna, the needs of her new son felt quite persecuting.

> I was so happy when he was born, but there were times when I couldn't help resenting him. He had colic and cried a lot in the first few weeks. Sometimes I would just think, "You're taking everything I have! What about *me*?" I dreaded each feed because my nipples were

cracked and bleeding, and I would have given everything I owned for just one night's sleep. One day he was crying and crying, I'd tried everything but he just wouldn't stop. I suddenly had this strong urge to throw him down the stairs, anything to stop that endless crying. It lasted a few seconds, but it was very strong. Afterwards I burst into tears. I was so worried, I had to hold on to him and rock him in my arms, telling him I was sorry, and that I loved him so much.

It is not unusual for mothers, and sometimes fathers too, to feel like this occasionally; even one of our best-loved lullabies involves a baby falling off a treetop. It can be lonely and frightening when these feelings are kept to ourselves, but they almost always become less powerful once they have been acknowledged. Even if we are worried about telling other people, we should be honest with ourselves, accepting that this is how it feels sometimes, even for the most loving parents. The very helplessness of a newborn baby can be hard to bear, especially when we are at our wits' end about how to make him feel better. Anger or resentment can be signals that we are becoming overwhelmed and need some time away from our baby, and ideally some looking after ourselves. If we feel that our own needs are being attended to, it will be much easier to rediscover our loving feelings towards the baby.

Of course there are times when these negative feelings become more worrying, and someone who feels they might really harm their baby will need to share their concerns straight away and get the support they need. But having occasional violent or aggressive impulses towards your baby does not alter the love you have for him. Feelings are not the same as actions. As Hanna's story shows, if we allow ourselves to feel the full depth of our negative feelings, whether in this or any other close relationship, it can help us to appreciate how strong our positive and loving feelings really are.

Milestones in the first six weeks

By the end of the first six weeks, the utter helplessness of the newborn has usually been replaced by a more robust baby, more aware of his surroundings and more able to relax and enjoy a bit more of what the world has to offer. The first real smile, when it comes, is a moment of exhilaration and pride for most parents. Sam recalls:

I remember feeling I was going to explode with happiness. I smiled at him and he just suddenly beamed back at me. I don't think I'd ever

felt such pure joy and excitement in my life. I was just tingling all
over. It was like falling in love.

For a very few parents, the first six weeks can be a calm and blissful time; for
most, it is a whirlwind of passions and anxieties. By the end of six weeks, most
mothers are feeling a bit more ready to venture out in the world – no longer
spending whole days in their dressing gowns, perhaps beginning to make
regular outings to the health visitor or meeting other mothers. The chaos is
beginning to find some shape. Parents can speak more confidently about their
baby's moods and preferences, times of day when he tends to be fretful, activi-
ties he enjoys and so on.

Once the baby has begun to hold his head up a little, and really recognize
his primary carers, is able to turn of his own accord towards the breast or
bottle or a familiar voice, can take in some of the noises and sights around him
as if they were beginning to make some kind of sense, can recognize feeding
time, enjoying both the food and the company, knowing that they belong to
him and that he belongs to the world – then for many parents the joy and
excitement of getting to know and love this growing baby, and being known
and loved in return, really begin.

3

Three to Six Months

New skills and new feelings

The next important stage in the baby's development is at three months. From about this age, the baby is beginning to feel much more in control. She enjoys her body more, discovering her hands and feet, reaching out to touch and hold things, experimenting with sounds and facial expressions. During the first few weeks of life, she related to things mostly through her mouth and eyes. When she was upset, she comforted herself by holding on to something with her eyes – a light, a toy, someone's eyes – or by holding on and sucking with her mouth. Once she can grasp with her hands, the world takes on a new meaning, although things tend to go straight into her mouth for a long time, to be properly inspected! A three-month-old being presented with a beautiful toy, or seeing a friendly face, will often show her enthusiasm by drooling or dribbling, before she thinks of stretching out a hand.

From three months the baby is becoming much more substantial and integrated. No longer helplessly preoccupied by whether or not her needs will be met, she is ready to explore the world. Jokes, games, conversations all become possible around this time. At this point, your baby smiling at you has a whole new meaning. She has become a person in her own right, and you have become a real person to her. It is wonderful to witness a baby becoming more at home in the world, beginning to enjoy the familiar, reliable experiences which are giving shape and pattern to her life.

Feeding: milk and what goes with it

Some mothers who have been breastfeeding move to bottles around this time, perhaps because they are returning to work, perhaps because they want a bit more freedom, or are not enjoying breastfeeding. Others find that breastfeeding becomes more enjoyable, now that both baby and mother are more confident and relaxed. Mothers who are bottle feeding usually find their babies are settling down to more of a rhythm, so feeds are easier to plan and become more enjoyable. Usually feeding is less tinged with anxieties about whether or not a baby is putting on enough weight, taking too much wind and so on.

Different personalities

Babies' individual temperaments and personalities continue to show themselves most vividly in their attitude towards food and feeding. The feeding relationship can be seen as a foundation for all future relationships, as it has been the baby's first real experience of taking something in – sustenance, love, comfort – from another person. It is also the arena in which the baby is beginning to work out where she ends and where her mother begins, exploring what it means to be two separate people, one giving and the other receiving.

Siobhan, at three months, left her mother in no doubt about her requirements around feeding. She would look eagerly for her mother's breast, latching on in a very passionate way. She focused on the breast with a determined expression, and once the milk came she would drink earnestly, her eyes shut.

> She always knew what was hers, what she was entitled to. It made me smile, because one of her hands would be sticking out into the air, middle finger and thumb together like a little gourmet diner. I always thought of her as saying, "Everything else in the world has to stop. I'm having my milk." And then afterwards, she would stretch out with her whole body, arms right up above her head and her eyes closed, completely satisfied.

Siobhan was a baby who claimed the breast and milk as her own and knew how to get the most pleasure and satisfaction out of her feeds. This was a source of great pleasure for her mother, too, who luckily didn't mind being allotted the role of observer rather than participant. Siobhan could enjoy a kind of fantasy that the breast and milk were hers and hers alone, so that even her mother ceased to exist for her while she was lost in her own blissful world.

For other babies, feeding is more obviously a give-and-take affair, and they enjoy the fact that their mother is sharing the experience with them. Clara was fed by breast and bottle from early on, and would gaze at her mother while feeding with a loving, trusting look.

> Sometimes when I offered her the milk she would just smile up at me for a while before she started feeding. Usually throughout a feed she kept her eyes fixed on mine, almost as if she was saying "thank you". And later on if I started chatting to my other children or watching TV while feeding her, she would break off and wait until she got my attention again.

Sometimes a feeding baby can seem like a little lover, passionate and adoring; sometimes she can appear quite comical, like the three-month-old who bashed herself in the face before feeds, due to her excited gesticulations on seeing the breast. One baby might be imperious and possessive, another hesitant and easily distracted. During this period, feeding remains a crucial focus in the baby's experience. Through the feeding relationship a baby is taking in not only milk, but also life itself, with all the richness this represents. Through the intimacy of the feeding relationship she is finding out what the world has to offer, and what it means to be so closely involved with another person.

The baby who rejects the breast

Of course, feeding at this age can still be an anxious business. Occasionally a baby who has been breastfed happily suddenly turns away from the breast at around this time, which can be bitterly disappointing for her mother. Carla's son, Ben, had been feeding well for the first three months or so, but then suddenly began to turn his face away, crying whenever she offered her breast.

> He would begin crying as soon as he saw the nipple. He seemed distressed and didn't want it, just turned his head away each time I tried. It was heartbreaking. I was going through a difficult patch in my relationship, and feeling pretty down, and I just kept thinking that he knew there was something different about me, something he didn't like, and he didn't want to be close to me any more.

Because breastfeeding is such an intimate part of the relationship, when a baby rejects her milk a mother can feel that it is she herself who is being rejected, especially if she is feeling vulnerable for other reasons. It can be difficult to get back her confidence. We can only speculate about what felt so wrong for Ben. Perhaps at the outset he was physically uncomfortable and didn't like the idea of feeding. Perhaps he did pick up something in his mother's altered mood and it upset him enough to turn away. Perhaps he was going through a difficult patch himself, and life was feeling all wrong, which meant mother was feeling all wrong – "life" and "mother" are not easily distinguishable for a three-month-old. Any of these factors could lead him to turn away from his feeds, feeling anxious or angry, needing to reject something that could be blamed for his horrible feelings.

It is very difficult to keep sight of the fact that sometimes our babies will see us as the "baddies", even when we feel we are doing the best we can by them. This is one of the most difficult of the many challenges we face as parents, and how well we can tolerate it depends very much on how robust we are feeling at the time.

Whatever caused the problem in Ben's feeding, it is clear that the more guilty and responsible Carla felt, the more difficult it was for the two of them to untangle the upset feelings on both sides and recover a more benign feeding relationship. After a week or two, having begun to supplement Ben's feed, Carla confided in a friend, and found it a great relief to talk to someone about her anxieties.

> I was so close to giving up, I was a bit panicky I think – maybe we'd both got a bit frightened. It did me good to talk to someone else who didn't see it as a complete disaster.

For Carla and Ben, a bit of encouragement from somebody outside the relationship was enough to help them resolve the problem. Carla expressed some milk for a couple of days, while he was refusing the breast, but felt less rejected, and Ben very soon began accepting her milk again. If he had been communicating some anger or frustration with his mother in turning away from her breast, it must have been a relief to Ben that she could tolerate such feelings, and continue to offer her milk with confidence that he would eventually come round.

Introducing solids

We have seen how much a baby's personality begins to develop and reveal itself in her relationship to breast and bottle feeding. When it comes to the next major step, trying solids for the first time, a whole new range of feelings and responses come into play. Even before the process begins, the question of when to introduce solids is much debated and can be an emotive issue. Parents often agonize over when to take the plunge, sometimes before and sometimes after the six-month mark; clearly it is a question not only of when a baby is physically ready, but also of when she is emotionally ready – not to mention when her mother is!

Sometimes anxieties over weaning emerge in worries about exactly what to give your baby, heightened concerns over hygiene or the detailed ingredients of every mouthful. Letting go of milk as the sole source of your baby's nutritional needs seems to stir up anxieties about whether the world is full of digestible or poisonous things – whether moving away from mummy is really going to be all right.

As with all new developments in a baby's life, weaning brings joys and losses. The word "weaning" means both "accustom to" and "encourage away from". This double meaning highlights the gains and losses of starting on solid food. Trying something new does mean letting go of the relationship as it was before, and is bound to stir up strong feelings about growth and separation. And parents have something to give up, too. The baby is no longer a suckling, fed in a close embrace. She is ready to take in food from a bit more of a distance, on a lap or a chair, and this is a significant change for all concerned.

But it is an exciting time too. For example, when a baby has been breast-fed, it can also be the first chance for her father, or for older siblings, to become involved in mealtimes. Harry was a third child and his older brothers couldn't wait for him to take solid food for the first time.

> In our house, Harry's first mouthful of baby rice was greeted as a cause for celebration. Suddenly everybody wanted to be involved in his feeds, and his brothers squabbled over who was allowed to hold the spoon. They loved the idea that he was getting more like them – and not so much of a mummy's boy. I felt a bit sad, though. He wasn't my baby any more, not in the same way. He was moving on.

Babies also differ in their reaction to this strange new world. Molly, for example, took to solid foods with great gusto, trying straight away to get hold of the spoon and get as much as she could, as if she had just been waiting for a chance to get started. Her only difficulty was that the spoon kept disappearing between mouthfuls, a concept which completely baffled and infuriated her.

But Harry, whose brothers were so eager for him to leave early infancy behind him, was not so sure.

> When it came to it, Harry looked at us as if we had gone mad. He reacted as if the spoon was some alien object, with this weird gungey stuff suddenly filling up his mouth. Most of it came straight out again, and I'll never forget the look of bafflement on his face: "That's not what I ordered!" He didn't understand it for a long time.

For some babies, a bit of encouragement is needed before they can get used to such a new way of doing things, and begin to take an interest in these new tastes and textures. Perhaps Harry, like his mother, was conscious of something having been lost, and this feeling needed to be given some time before the advantages began to dawn on him.

As with all new challenges, it is hard to process all the meanings at once, and how we deal with growing up and moving on is a deep part of our personalities. For Harry, moving on to solids meant giving up what he knew and loved; he wasn't sure he wanted to move on, grow up or let go so easily. Regret, sadness and loss often take their place along with relief, pleasure and pride in each developmental stage. But now that there is a bit more distance during feeds, we can begin to share the experience with our babies in a new way. There is a new dimension to the process, new tools which both adult and baby are using, new discoveries about what tastes nice and what doesn't, a new space between them to experience together how the food comes and goes.

Becoming more separate

Weaning onto solid food marks one significant shift in the early closeness between mother or father and baby. The baby's new confidence and new skills can now lead her to make a whole range of other new forays into the world. Again, the mother–baby relationship is becoming a little bit less exclusive and some of the early closeness lessens; but the scope for mutual enjoyment and the sharing of new experiences seems to be endlessly widening, and this can feel like a coming together as much as a moving apart.

A baby of a few months old can now focus much more readily on things that are further away, and she is able to choose what she looks at. Early versions of peekaboo are now possible, as the comings and goings of siblings, toys, parents, even pets, become more interesting and meaningful to the baby.

As she begins to recognize and appreciate mother, father, siblings and grand-parents, she also seems more able to recognize her own feelings. Her mind is becoming more focused and she is working at making sense of how things feel.

Emma, at three months, was seen under a much-loved animal mobile, watching intently as one particular animal came into view then disappeared again. Whenever it appeared she beamed with pleasure, but as it floated out of sight she exclaimed angrily, kicking her legs vigorously, protesting at its departure. Emma seemed to be using the mobile to express and explore some of her feelings about comings and goings, what she liked and what made her angry. Even at this age, babies are using play to make sense of their feelings.

Sleeping

Over the first few months, most parents struggle with the exhausting process of persuading a new baby that night-time really is meant for sleep. Even when this has been achieved with at least some degree of success, issues around bedtime and sleeping continue to preoccupy many parents. Sleep is also linked with separation, and can be just as emotional an area for parents as it is for babies and children.

To begin with, many parents decide to make changes in sleeping arrangements at some point during this period, perhaps moving the baby into her own Moses basket or cot, or into her own room. This can be part of a drive to establish new boundaries between the baby and her parents and it can take a lot of negotiation and renegotiation before things settle into place. We can become very identified with how our baby feels – or how we *think* she is going to feel – when we impose such boundaries. It is all too easy to attribute all sorts of responses to our baby which might have their origins in our own personalities as much as in hers.

Sue and Dylan, first-time parents, had put Matthew in his Moses basket at the end of their bed until he was four months old. Matthew was a very good sleeper and usually didn't need feeding at night. Sue, however, was finding it hard to get to sleep with Matthew so close to her, conscious of his every move and snuffle. Both Sue and Dylan felt that they needed a bit of time and space away from Matthew in the night-time. They had recently moved house, and the room they moved Matthew into was still in a shabby condition. The first night they moved him in, he woke up three times in the night, very distressed, and Sue found it difficult to get him back to sleep.

This pattern continued for the next week, and both Sue and Dylan felt bitterly disappointed, and puzzled as to why Matthew suddenly found it difficult to sleep. He had recently started on solid food, and they wondered whether this was what was unsettling him. When they sat down and talked about it, they realized that both of them were feeling guilty and worried about moving Matthew out of the parental bedroom. They had both been feeling upset to think of him all on his own, imagining that he must feel unloved and unwanted. Sue confessed that she hated the new room and had been sitting with Matthew during his night feeds, staring at the shabby walls feeling utterly miserable.

What seemed to be happening was that these parents' own feelings about Matthew being banished from their bedroom were affecting his responses to the new set-up. If they didn't believe Matthew's own room could be a nice place to be, they didn't stand much chance of convincing him! After Sue and Dylan were able to talk to one another about their anxieties, and about how churned up they both felt about Matthew's move into the new room, Dylan put a couple of pictures up above Matthew's cot, and both parents began to feel a bit calmer about things. To their relief, putting Matthew to bed in his new room at once became easier. Within two nights, he had resumed sleeping through the nights – and his parents were able to enjoy having their own room back again.

Obviously the two pictures in themselves wouldn't matter much to Matthew, but perhaps they were important for what they represented for his parents – the idea that this new development could have real benefits for Matthew, not just losses. It is never possible to completely untangle which feeling about a new separation originates with the baby and which with his parents; there will always be a bit of both. But it can help to try to tease out where our own feelings might be clouding our perception of our baby's. There are many things a baby will have to find out for herself, through direct experience; and one of these is that the gradual stages of moving away from one's parents can feel sad and lonely, but can also offer new opportunities and new pleasures.

"Controlled crying"

The parents' point of view

Most parents find themselves wondering at some stage about the pros and cons of putting their babies down and letting them cry for a bit before they eventually go to sleep – the process which is known rather coldly as "controlled crying". In this area, as in so many where separations are involved, feelings run high. Just as some people are horrified at this idea, imagining it must involve being callously "controlling" of your baby, leaving her to cry herself to sleep, others go just as far the other way, judging parents who pick up and comfort their babies throughout the night as hopelessly indulgent, unable to control their own desire to run straight to the crying baby, thereby "making a rod for their own backs". Each camp eyes the other with suspicion, perhaps tinged with self-doubt; parents feel they have to get this right, but are usually unsure about what all of this means for the baby.

This leads back to what happened when Matthew moved into his new room. It seems probable that Matthew picked up on the way that his parents were feeling as they put him to bed each night. So there must be something about the way in which we place our babies into their cots, kiss them goodnight, or speak to them, which transmits messages to them about our deepest feelings. And if we really believe this, then the whole question of whether or not controlled crying works hinges just as much on our own personalities, our own feelings about this separation, as on the merits of the system itself. If we can convince a baby that we feel confident in what we are doing, that we really believe each separation is going to be manageable, this method stands a much better chance of working. Getting to this point, though, is easier said than done.

As adults, many of us find it easier to deal with our anxieties during the day than at night-time. Some of us might remember being frightened of the dark as children, having nightmares or feeling lonely and anxious all alone. And faced with our baby's night-time distress or anxieties, many of us will find it much more difficult to keep a grip on our adult perspective, which might have come to our rescue during daylight hours.

Sally was bringing up her daughter, Tia, on her own. She had enjoyed having Tia in her bed, where she could comfort her and be close to her throughout the night. But when Tia was five months old, she decided to move her into her own cot. Tia was not impressed, and cried angrily when Sally put her down, then became increasingly distressed as she was still not returned to her mother's side. Sally found Tia's reaction heartbreaking, but she felt that she had made her decision and needed to stick with it. Controlled crying had sounded like a sensible idea. But as the night went on and Tia cried so miserably, Sally found she literally couldn't bear it, and began to feel convinced that Tia was going to be damaged for life if she was left in such a terrible state. Sally felt she had no choice but to let Tia come back to the bed, where she settled down at once. Sally was left feeling like a failure, and angry that no one had told her how difficult it would be.

This sort of situation is very common. Dealing with a crying baby during the night must be one of the most challenging tasks for all parents, and even more difficult to manage on your own. Two parents together have the potential to provide some support for one another, helping each other to hold on during the more turbulent patches – as long as in their exhaustion they don't take it out on each other. But even with support, to hear your baby crying, when you know that you could make her feel better if only you would pick her up, or take her back to bed with you, or give her an extra feed, and yet force yourself not to do it, can seem against nature and intuition.

As we have seen, most babies do need help with putting some sort of boundary around their feelings. A baby has very basic ideas about herself, and cannot possibly know whether she is ready to cope with a new stage of separation or not, although she is likely to assume not. As parents, we don't yet know what she is capable of either, but we have the benefit of our own experience, and a longer-term perspective on her growing strengths. It is hard, especially in the middle of the night, not to identify with the feelings of the crying baby so much that we become caught up in her perspective and lose touch with our own.

Sally eventually consulted her health visitor, who suggested a step-by-step regime for managing the night-time crying. To Sally's relief, this included being able to comfort and reassure her baby each step of the way, and never leaving her for longer than she could manage, while holding firmly to the principle of not giving in to her desire to be back in bed with her mother. With the backing of her health visitor, Sally found that she didn't feel so cruel about saying "No" to Tia's demands, and Tia eventually accepted the new rules – although not without a fight!

Sometimes we need to work at being the grown-up for our baby, understanding fully that she might feel desperate and frightened, but gently insisting that we are not desperate and frightened ourselves. It is difficult, and most of us will need some outside support to do this, but it can make a real difference. For both baby and parents, the knowledge that not *everybody* is in the grip of these infantile feelings – that we really, genuinely have faith that there is nothing to be so frightened about, and that things will get better – can make night-time anxieties around separation much more manageable.

The baby's point of view

If we imagine the whole process from a baby's point of view, it must feel shocking to her when we leave her to cry, even for a few minutes. A baby who is feeling upset, wanting her mummy to pick her up, cuddle or feed her, is bound to have strong reactions to her walking away. Depending on her personality and what the relationship is like, she might feel indignant, angry, panicky, bewildered – any number of feelings – but something bad is definitely happening. Often this bad feeling builds up as time passes and her mother still hasn't come back.

If her parents are leaving her for small amounts of time, she is faced with the task, bit by bit, of trying to find resources within herself to deal with the situation. Early on she might quite quickly begin to feel panicky when mother isn't there, even for a very short time, and she really does need her physical presence before things can feel all right again. By the time she is a few months old, she is usually ready to begin the gradual process of testing out what she can do to feel a bit better while her mother is away. As long as she isn't left too soon, she can begin using her own thoughts and memories to help her through.

A baby would like us to appear at the first sign of distress, to give her whatever she needs for immediate comfort and gratification. But knowing that we are close by, and will not leave her to deal with her upset feelings on her own for too long too soon, she will begin to find that she can comfort herself even when we aren't there. This cannot be achieved all at once, and at times she will become frightened and feel that she can't do it. That is why we need to be sensitive and in touch with her feelings, returning as often as we need to, reassuring her that she is still all right, that we are still there, and that nothing so terrible is going to happen. Most parents can tell an indignant, protesting sort of cry from a desperate or panicky one, so she will quickly learn that mummy or daddy do come if she is really in a state.

If she senses that we are in touch with what she is going through, but have faith that she will come out the other side, a baby is more likely to discover through her own experience that this is true. One of the hardest tasks of parenthood is helping our babies to learn that distress, anger or loneliness are not things that threaten their survival, however much they feel like that at the time. Even a baby who has been beside herself with misery and rage during the night can wake up the next morning and give you a beaming smile.

The developing baby

By the end of six months, some babies are beginning to sit up on their own, most have begun to widen their circle of loved ones, their repertoire of voices and expressions, and their interest in the world. They appear to have the world at their feet, and can display a sense of self-importance and imperiousness which are touching and endearing. For fathers, grandparents and older siblings, this is a very exciting time, as the baby is ready to develop deeper and more meaningful relationships with each of them, appreciating that each is different and offers various pleasures and interests.

A baby of six months is much more aware of her feelings. She can become absolutely furious; she can also be deeply loving and affectionate. But the early, primitive view of the world is giving way to much more sophisticated, complex feelings. The baby is beginning to think for herself. She can enjoy being alone, lying in her cot enraptured by a mobile or the view from a window. She can recognize when she is hungry, nicely full up, angry with mummy, loving towards granny, excited by a new discovery, worried about being left, and so on. No longer so bewildered by the newness of life, no longer at the mercy of chaotic feelings or happenings which spring out from nowhere, she has a secure base around her, and growing resources inside. She can begin to make forays into the world armed with increased confidence and self-assurance.

4

Six to Twelve Months

The second half of a baby's first year sees a complete transformation. The infant who can still explore the world only as it is brought directly into his reach or line of vision, turns into a mobile and adventurous little person with plans and ideas of his own. Many parents find this period one of the most enjoyable yet. Your baby is beginning to show his appreciation of life in his excited response to all the new skills he is collecting, and a growing capacity to express enjoyment, humour and affection. He can also make very effective protests when something displeases him.

As we saw earlier, in the first stage of a baby's life the parents' and baby's emotions are so closely entwined that it is virtually impossible to be sure whose is whose: each is intensely affected by the other. By this stage, babies have learnt a lot more about their own feelings, and are developing the capacity to notice that those around them have feelings too. They have all along been deeply affected by their parents' states of mind without consciously *knowing* about them. Now that they have a sense of themselves as people, they are beginning very slowly to observe, learn and think about other people's moods and behaviour. The stage is being set for much more complex, challenging and rewarding relationships.

The baby becomes more integrated

The powerful and extreme states of mind of early infancy, with all its ups and downs, will continue to make an impact throughout the first year of the baby's life and beyond. However, the simplistic and extreme quality of his perceptions has already altered, and he has a more established sense of himself. During the second half of his first year he is becoming more able to integrate his thoughts and feelings, giving him a more coherent and more subtle view of himself and others.

Seeing himself in a new light

At first, a tiny baby seems to perceive all the good and bad feelings as coming from some unknown force outside of himself: when he is hungry, tired, lonely, in pain, he looks as though bad things are being *done to him*. You can see a baby of a few weeks old looking at you in terror, as if he really feels he is being attacked – whether by a stab of colic, a panicky feeling or a sudden hunger. But as he faces the task of getting to know himself better, he has a dawning awareness that not all good or bad feelings come from outside of himself – that he has "good" and "bad" feelings inside him, too. He can feel aggression and rage, as well as love and affection. Feeling less passive, more in control and more of an individual, he will gradually join the rest of humanity as he struggles with his own limitations, his unlikeable or destructive impulses, his basic humanness.

Seeing his mother in a new light

At about the same time as he is making these discoveries about himself, the baby is going to be faced with the realization that his mother, and father too, are also complex and flawed beings. As we saw earlier, a tiny baby can have no possible concept of his mother as a separate person with good and bad qualities. She is not a person at all, she is essentially his whole world, whether this means something wonderful, when she is there, giving him what he needs, or something terrible, when she is not there, or not taking away his bad feelings. Gradually, now, the baby is discovering that his mother is a whole, separate person, someone who has all sorts of different characteristics, who can provide love, nourishment, laughter, but who can also be offish or prickly, or fail to understand his needs: a being who might change from moment to moment but somehow remains the same person.

All of these discoveries present a huge challenge for the baby, and at times the growing complexity of his relationships can feel quite painful and worrying. He is losing the illusion of a perfect, all-providing mother. That perfect creature whom he has gazed at with such unadulterated love and devotion, who admittedly disappeared sometimes, or was replaced by a nastier version when things were going wrong, nevertheless represented a version of "mummy" that is hard to give up. Perceiving that he has a three-dimensional mother might be preferable in the long term, but it can also bring disappointment and threaten his equilibrium. Most babies will find ways to filter this experience if it becomes too difficult, summoning up the idealized mother when the going gets tough.

In the midst of all these changes, the baby can feel quite overwhelmed and needs us to keep some boundaries for him. With our greater experience and our sympathy, we can give him a language to understand these new feelings. If we can also be firm and consistent we are also showing him that there are limits around the "dangers" he is beginning to perceive – both in the external world and within his own imagination.

Acquiring teeth

As if these challenges weren't enough, the baby will usually acquire his first teeth during this period. Many babies find teething physically painful and become very fretful and miserable. But the arrival of teeth must require some major readjustments on an emotional level, too. Just as the baby is discovering that he and other people possess sharper, more aggressive qualities, he is faced with the sudden intrusion of hard, sharp objects in his mouth, where all has been soft before. And because his mouth has always been such an important part of him, the place where he explores, feeds and cries, this change is bound to stir up strong and confusing feelings. The sucking impulse no longer holds sway; he becomes preoccupied by chewing, and you often see a teething baby almost compulsively pressing objects against his new teeth with a serious, worried look. It may be some time before he adjusts to all this strangeness and discomfort, and can begin to enjoy the advantages of biting, with all its many uses.

Loneliness

Now that he is so much more aware of his mother as a separate person, for the first time the baby begins to understand what it is like to feel "left out', realizing with a stab of jealousy that the people he loves have other relationships that exclude him. It is dawning on him that his mother talks to his father in a different way, that they get together when *he* wants their attention. Siblings get together without his permission, too, perhaps after he has been put to bed. Friends visit and occupy everyone's attention, talking and laughing together in ways he doesn't understand. He might respond robustly, trying to join in, laughing or babbling along so that he feels included. But sometimes he will feel angry or anxious about being left out. He might suddenly begin protesting at bedtime, or wake during the night, not wanting to be left alone. He might seem wary of certain visitors, seeing them more as unwanted intruders rather than simply more people to play with. He might take to loud shouting whenever his mother is having a conversation with someone else.

Some parents notice a new quality of sadness in their babies at times over this period. Perhaps there are moments when we see a look of thoughtfulness, even melancholy, or hear a more subdued kind of crying. There is now a sense that the baby misses his mother or father when they are absent, and is keenly aware of other people's comings and goings.

The importance of playing

While so much is happening in your baby's emotional world, he is also surging ahead with his physical and intellectual growth, experimenting and exploring with boundless curiosity. Some time around six or seven months he will probably sit up unaided for the first time. This marks an important shift into a more upright, sociable phase of his life, and his fascination with the world around him really takes off. Many babies during this period enjoy having a box of objects placed in front of them, a "treasure chest" from which they can draw out bits and pieces that interest them – test how things feel against their teeth or gums, place one thing next to, inside or around another thing, see if they can fit or bang things together, working out how they can make things happen.

Play is absolutely crucial to the developing baby. Just as he is picking up certain objects, putting them together, one inside the other, or crashing them together to see what happens, so, through his play, he is picking his way through different feelings, relationships and interactions, finding out what makes things happen, what produces which response, how it feels when people behave in certain ways. Life is much less frightening and bewildering when you can digest it bit by bit, in your own time, in ways which make sense to you. The classic example is the game of peekaboo, which allows a child to experiment with the emotive area of partings and reunions in a controlled, manageable setting. Other people's absences and returns; loud noises, or sudden shouting; a child's face suddenly appearing and disappearing; a family cat who pounces; an unexpected, loving kiss; a whole array of experiences which have been confusing and out of his control, are gradually brought into his sphere of investigation as he pores and puzzles over them like a little scientist, just as he is doing with his toys.

Engaging with the world, and provoking a response

Babies of six months and upwards are much more engaged with the world outside, and eager to interact with other people, although they might prefer doing so when a parent is close at hand. They are beginning to understand words, and to play at talking themselves, delighted by the response this provokes: first they will vocalize and imitate sounds, later moving on to "pretend" talk, or babbling. They are learning that they have a role to play, that they can have an impact on people and make things happen. Just as pushing buttons on a toy or knocking over a tower of bricks have an immediate effect, babies are learning that their behaviour can have an impact on those around them – though usually not in quite such a dramatic way. For as well as playing with the feelings and experiences *they* are having, babies of this age are beginning to notice other people's moods, and to experiment with how they can provoke particular responses.

The earliest way in which a baby provokes a response is through his crying. A newborn baby cries involuntarily, having no conscious means of influencing the behaviour of the adults around him; he has an impulse to rid himself of physical pain, or painful feelings. But he quickly learns that crying can make things happen. A baby of six months or more is a much more subtle creature, and is very gradually learning to observe how his behaviour influences those caring for him, and how to respond accordingly. Even at seven or eight months, a baby whose mother is feeling tired can learn to find ways to "cheer her up", working to discover which games or funny antics might make her seem happier. Similarly, a father whose mind is on other things for a while can suddenly find himself with a particularly active or reckless baby, who has found a way to summon up an urgent need for attention. In this way babies are working out that parents' moods do vary, and puzzling out what they can do about all of this, discovering that there are some things they can control or have some influence on, and some things they can't.

George, at nine months, developed an ear-splitting scream which had an immediate effect on everyone in the vicinity. When the family had moved into a new flat and were particularly concerned not to annoy their new neighbours, his father John describes how George developed his technique still further. He began to wake up several times each night, so that one of his parents had to go and attend to him. He would then scream his most piercing scream as soon as they tried to leave his room.

> He would shriek with all his might, almost deafening me and probably the whole street, too – and then stop, look at me with a cheerful expression, knowing full well there wasn't a thing I could do to stop him.

It may be that George was originally waking up genuinely needing reassurance in his new surroundings. But his very deliberate, well-placed screams obviously gave him a wonderful opportunity to wield some power over his parents. Babies have a way of getting under our skins, making us feel uncomfortable or unsettled when that is how *they* are feeling. George might not have any control over which house his parents moved into, but he could let his parents know what it feels like when somebody else has all the power – and he had a flair for it. Infuriating as it was, George's parents were just about able to see the humour in the situation. When it got too much they decided to brazen it out (after having a word with the neighbours) and after a few nights George settled down again, having made his point.

Laughter and jokes

Just as a baby like George finds ways to assert his power at times, of course there are times when a baby needs to know that he can elicit something softer. Becky, at ten months, knew how to provoke laughter and kisses from her parents by lying on her back and kicking her legs vigorously, like a small baby. Even very young babies can look highly amused by their parents' or older siblings' strange antics, and by this age as well as knowing how to entertain others, they appreciate surprisingly sophisticated jokes, absurd situations and games.

Laughter and playing are a central part of the baby's life. Hearing your baby laugh for the first time is a thrilling experience. He now has a sense of his own innate ability to please, to be loved, to laugh and make other people laugh. Sharing games with his mother and others also highlights the fact that the mother–baby relationship is no longer so intense, based on needs which must be met, nor is it so exclusive. More relaxed, the baby can enjoy his mother's and other people's company in a whole host of new and exciting ways.

Triumphs and disasters

In the second half of his first year the baby is continually trying to build up a picture of the people who matter most to him and, as we have seen, he is simultaneously building up a picture of himself. At this age, achieving anything like a rational, balanced view of his own powers and limitations is well beyond him. In fact, he is likely to be full of strong and conflicting beliefs about himself, varying from delusions of complete omnipotence to pangs of real helplessness. It is not so long ago that he was utterly tiny and dependent. But as he learns about the genuine strengths inside him, he can quickly magnify this strength until he becomes powerful beyond all proportion in his own mind. These lurches between strength and vulnerability can be very confusing, and the gap between how strong he imagines himself to be, and the limits of what he can actually achieve, leaves him in a delicate position.

Self-importance

Nobody can appear as regal or all-powerful as a baby at the height of his self-importance. Bouncing on a swing suspended from the door frame in the middle of his parents' sitting room, knowing he is the centrepiece, the absolute centre of attention. Learning the joys of pointing – those wonderful moments when adults obey his commands, with orders such as "Da!" which bring the object of his desire quickly into his grasp. Handing out selected toys to a roomful of adults, having no doubt that any adult he chooses to bestow something on will accept with great thanks and deference. Holding out his hands to be picked up, with complete trust that he will be obeyed. All of this makes for a glorious feeling of omnipotence. Babies of this age know how to feel powerful, how to shrug off all knowledge of their neediness, how to enjoy moments of complete domination.

And collapse

But falling from such great heights of omnipotence is a long way to fall. The baby who can feel that he has the world at his feet, is the same baby who is unable to pick up a drink which is just millimetres out of reach. He can find himself on his arms, beaming proudly, enjoying the encouraging applause and admiration from onlookers, as he struggles to bear the weight of his upper body. But after a considerable effort, his arms give way and he falls flat on his face; he is left lying on his tummy, unable to move. Sometimes he might find himself making for a favourite toy someone has put just out of his reach, only to find he can manage backwards but not forwards. Or even taking those first miraculous steps, with rising euphoria all round – after which the carpet changes direction abruptly, and he is suddenly landing with a bump to the back of his head.

Life for a baby is full of such extremes. So much is there to be achieved, and so many new pleasures to be had, but there are a relentless number of pitfalls on the way. It requires a very delicate process of trial and error, hanging on to his sense of self in the face of triumphs and disasters coming in quick succession. A baby of six months and over may not consciously remember his early infancy, but such experiences of helplessness must hit on a raw nerve, as somewhere inside him he still knows what it is like to be tiny, and utterly dependent on other people for his survival. In many ways, all that is far behind him. But it will never leave him altogether. When very hungry, lonely or frightened, even much older babies (not to mention adults) can still seem to disintegrate for a little while, as if reliving the panicky feelings of early infancy when an empty mouth longs for a nipple or teat but is absolutely powerless to make it come. Babies of this age are still working very hard to sustain their sense of who they are – somewhere between this very helpless state and the perilous joys of being "on top of the world".

Parental responses

Watching someone you love going through these lurches can be very endearing – or very comical, or very excruciating, depending on the situation. A great deal also depends on our own capacity to bear frustration, and how much we can allow ourselves, not just our babies, to be human. However we struggle with our own feelings as we watch our baby's triumphs and humiliations, he will be needing a great deal of sensitivity and careful handling from us.

The baby's need to feel powerful

From the beginning of our baby's life, one of our roles is to provide an environment where he can feel in control sometimes, where food does come when he cries, where toys are within reach, where it is possible for him to feel powerful, even omnipotent, sometimes. Babies need to have experiences like this, right from the start, so that they can build up their strength and inner confidence. For example, a baby as young as three months can get great pleasure when he is allowed to play with the nipple or teat after or during a feed, letting it in and out of his mouth, proving that he can get it back when he wants. And for most mothers these are precious and touching moments, too. We know instinctively that a baby needs to experience this feeling, and that he can't deal with too much frustration or helplessness at once.

The need for boundaries

However, as he is so susceptible to allowing genuine power to tip over into the dizzy heights of omnipotence, a baby also needs proof that we are *not* going to let his powers go unchecked, however hard he might push at the limits.

Jack, at eleven months, would put his hand on the television and look expectantly at his mother, waiting for the word "No" to come. When it did, he would laugh excitedly, his whole body dancing with pleasure, and within a few minutes he would reach out his hand again, waiting for the familiar response. Like with most games, at least part of the pleasure is in knowing what the rules are, seeing the expected response happening each time, as the tension is resolved.

Perhaps Jack, like many babies of this age, also liked to prove to himself that his mother could be relied upon to assert boundaries and rules, giving him a feeling of safety. Although babies, like older children and adolescents, often protest and keep pushing at boundaries, they tend to be relieved when the boundary holds. We should always take a baby's anger and outrage seriously. But just as we help him put a boundary around his more vulnerable feelings, we also need to let him know that however angry he gets, or how powerful he feels, we will *not* let him topple us over. Being the boss might seem like a good idea at the time, but if a baby begins to think he really might have complete power over us, he will quickly become anxious. We need to provide him with a safe arena in which to experiment with his wilder feelings and impulses, knowing there is somebody there to stop him if he goes too far.

Encouraging growth

With the older baby, we have our own transition to negotiate. We have become accustomed to providing and bringing into reach things we know he wants, responding to his need to be imperious and having his orders obeyed at least some of the time. Increasingly, our role will involve introducing new challenges. With the older baby we need to stretch and encourage him a bit more, to put the ball just out of reach when he is learning to crawl, to leave him for a bit when he is frustrated with a toy which won't do what he wants. He may look at us with indignation, but usually he will appreciate it when he finds that he can actually make the connection himself. Very gently we can help him to learn that bearing frustration, and a certain amount of distress, can be manageable, and that he really does have internal resources to help him through. We are allowing him the excitement of thinking for himself, seeing what he can do when we leave him to his own devices.

Surprisingly often, someone other than the baby's mother assumes the role of stretching him that little bit further, encouraging him to take risks, to achieve something on his own, to venture out into the world, away from mummy. Mothers are sometimes more ambivalent about their babies' new departures, more protective, perhaps holding on to the more vulnerable aspect of their personalities; while fathers can be more teasing, their play at times more robust, more challenging. These different roles represent the ever-present tension between the pull to stay close and safe with mummy forever, and the lure of the outside world, represented by "daddy" or another third party; the world of adventure, risk-taking and increasing independence.

The baby's resourcefulness

It is impressive how much babies of this age will tolerate, and how they continue to be driven towards new developmental stages even when they fail again and again. Some babies are more persistent or tenacious in pursuing their goals, dealing with the accompanying doses of frustration and impatience. Others appear more relaxed about moving on, perhaps temperamentally less driven, lingering over each stage for a bit longer until they are absolutely ready. While their parents might be waiting eagerly for them to reach each new milestone, they seem content to go at their own pace.

Babies can also prove very good at distracting themselves if something goes wrong. If one skill proves unattainable, some babies will quickly find something they know they *can* do. At nine months, Leah was seen making heroic efforts to crawl, but having no success, and was becoming frustrated and demoralized. Rather than giving in to tears, she suddenly pointed to a toy that was within her reach, and clasped it to her with a cry of joy, as if this is what she'd wanted all along. In a similar way, a baby who is having problems with one parent might turn his attention to the other, or to an aunt or family friend, or even to a complete stranger, in order to make the best of things.

These impulses can be very helpful, the beginnings of the capacity to "make do" with what you've got, at least enough to tide you over during a difficult patch. Naturally we don't expect or want our babies to try to avoid all frustrations and all difficulties by turning away – but a bit of time off can be very restorative.

One of the most impressive and touching thing about babies is their ability to forgive both objects and people who do let them down. A toy which has been very troublesome and has been shouted at in rage, can a few moments later be picked up and given a loving embrace.

Parental expectations and peer groups

It is easy to become so identified with our children that their successes seem to reflect glory onto us, and their collapses make us feel like failures. Some babies seem more ambitious than others, and it goes without saying that some parents are temperamentally more ambitious too, and have higher expectations for their children, whether they mean to or not. There cannot be many parents who haven't found themselves pushing their babies onwards towards new skills and milestones, so that they can catch up with or surpass their peers – even when the baby doesn't seem particularly concerned.

At nine months, Georgia had shown no interest whatsoever in moving from her favourite position, sitting. Her mother Sylvia took her to a mother and baby group every now and then, and on one visit realized that every other baby in the group was now able to move, either crawling or bottom shuffling.

> We put our babies down at our feet, and were sitting there chatting, and before I knew it, the other four babies had simply gone off. Georgia was left all on her own, sitting there playing with the toys in front of her. I suddenly had this strong feeling, almost like shame: "Why can't my baby do that? What's wrong with her?" I knew that Georgia was as happy as ever, playing away and she hadn't even noticed. But it really got to me.

On reflection, perhaps Sylvia was really recalling moments from her own life when she felt suddenly left behind, watching others move on while she was left feeling like a failure. Responses such as this can surge up inside any of us, when we might think we are empathizing with our babies, but it would be closer to the truth to say we are empathizing with some aspect of our childhood selves.

It is hard to accept and to remain in touch with all aspects of our baby – the powerful, imperious creature who bosses us about, as well as the collapsed, defeated infant who just needs to be held. Something in a bossy baby might suddenly remind us of a trait we dislike in ourselves, leaving us more irritated than usual. Or, if we suddenly feel intolerant of our baby's "clinginess", we might find that there is some area of vulnerability in ourselves that we would rather not be reminded of. It can be very complicated when we think we recognize something of ourselves writ large in the personalities of our offspring. And the strength of our own feelings can obscure the fact that our babies might feel completely differently, having strengths and weaknesses that are uniquely their own.

5

Coping with Separation

Returning to Work and Weaning from the Breast

Some time during the first year, sometimes later, many mothers return to work, and many stop breastfeeding. Sometimes the two are connected, when breastfeeding is no longer possible due to working hours, and sometimes the two decisions are made separately. How the baby reacts to such major changes depends on many things, including her age, how resilient she is temperamentally, how secure she feels in her relationship with her mother and father, how well she has coped with earlier losses or separations, and how much capacity she has (and whether she is ready) for forming genuine attachments to people other than her mother.

Of course, a great deal also depends on the circumstances and personality of the mother, and how much she is able to rally her own resources to help her baby with the challenges ahead. A great deal is asked of a mother at these times. Can she keep her confidence in doing the right thing, while remaining open to the very needy, infantile feelings which her baby might be communicating to her? Can she sympathize with her baby's feelings of loss or anger, bearing the pain on her behalf, while simultaneously managing her own feelings of regret, sadness or guilt? Will she find herself skating over the difficulties, seeking to cheer herself or her baby up too soon, rather than letting her be miserable or angry for a while? Particularly if she is returning to work, is she ready to let go of her baby a bit more, allowing other people to become close to her and to share the intimate experiences of feeding, cleaning, cuddling and playing with her?

Transitions such as these do involve loss, and will never be achieved without some sadness, anger and anxiety on both sides. However, neither experience needs to be traumatic, as long as it is handled sensitively. If the baby's parents are able to remain in touch with themselves and with their baby, letting her see that her feelings will be accepted and understood, she will learn that change and loss are painful, but manageable – and that they can yield new opportunities, too.

Returning to work

When a mother returns to work, there is almost always a degree of guilt around, and sometimes a prodigious amount. There can be very different kinds of guilt. A woman who is forced to return to work against her will may be wracked with guilt in a completely different way from someone who has chosen to go back to work and actually wants a bit of time away from her baby. How well we deal with our guilt also depends a good deal on how supported we are, by the baby's father, by parents or friends, or by colleagues at work, and by whoever will be looking after the baby in our absence. All of these people can help keep things in perspective and provide vital reassurance that we are still good mothers, and that our babies will be all right.

Babies go through phases of being more dependent on their mothers for comfort, and often it can feel as though the time when your baby needs you most is the time when you need to return to work. Sometimes this might be true (and this will be mentioned later), but again, our own feelings about separation will influence our view of how our babies are going to cope, and it can be very difficult to keep sight of when the anxieties really originate with the baby.

Difficulties saying goodbye

Jenny, who went back to work part-time when Helen was seven months old, found the moment of parting difficult to bear, and thought it best to slip quietly away without having to face Helen's reaction to her leaving. But when Helen noticed her mother had gone, she became distraught, crying inconsolably for over an hour. She also began waking up again in the night, needing an extra feed and a great deal of comforting. Eventually the childminder suggested that Jenny tried saying goodbye to Helen directly, even if it meant facing a barrage of tears. Jenny reluctantly tried this, looking Helen in the eye, waving and saying goodbye when it was time to go. Helen did cry very bitterly as she watched her mother leave, and Jenny stood outside listening, in tears herself. But to her surprise, within a few minutes Helen had calmed down and was allowing the childminder to settle her with some toys and a drink.

In trying to manage the separation from her daughter, Jenny was probably trying to shield herself, as well as Helen, from the dreaded moment of "goodbye". In fact, Helen seemed to feel more panicky when she was not informed of her mother's imminent departure. Babies of all ages look for patterns, links and meanings which make their world more predictable and therefore more manageable. Sudden changes or absences, which they are not given a chance to prepare for, make life feel more chaotic again, more like when they were tiny babies and bewildered much of the time. Even younger babies who don't understand "goodbye" yet will pick up on other clues surprisingly soon – perhaps the waving, cuddles or the particular tone of voice which herald their mothers' departure. Being kept more in the picture about separations and reunions can help them to pace themselves, as they become not only familiar with the pangs of parting, but also increasingly secure in the knowledge that mummy will come back.

Perhaps Helen, like most babies, could also manage her mother's absence better once she had been given the chance to express her anger or distress directly in Jenny's presence, knowing that her mother was really taking on board how she felt, not leaving her to deal with it on her own. This can be much more difficult for a mother to deal with – and no wonder it is tempting to slip away, especially when we are feeling churned up too. If we can muster up the courage to face these turbulent feelings rather than avoiding them, we are giving ourselves and our babies the chance to go through something difficult but very important, and discovering that we can manage just about all right. And babies also feel relieved when they find that their parents can bear the full force of their angry or upset feelings – that we will try to accept and understand them, even when things are tough for both of us.

A mother feels rejected

Sean's mother, Claire, returned to work part-time when Sean was eight months old. She enjoyed work, but had been dreading the moment when she would have to leave Sean, and full of guilt about what this would mean to him.

In fact, Sean was upset when she left him, but was enjoying his time with the new childminder. Claire had stopped breastfeeding Sean when he was four months old, as she had not really been enjoying it, and had always felt guilty about this, too. When he began taking solid food she took it as an opportunity to "make amends" to Sean, spending much time concocting dishes which he loved, and feeding became a special time that they enjoyed together.

About a week after her return to work Claire noticed that Sean was turning his nose up at food which he had previously loved.

> I remember one morning I'd made a whole batch of parsnip and sweet potato, which he adored. When I gave him the first mouthful he opened his mouth in readiness. But as soon as he tasted the food he winced and looked shocked, turning away as if it was the most disgusting thing he had ever tasted. He chewed on it for a while with his expression changing one minute to the next, keeping me in suspense. I stood there waiting, saying, "Yes? No? Yes? Do you like that?" He broke into a smile, and began to gurgle happily. I was relieved, and we seemed all right again. But after a few minutes he suddenly made a loud raspberry sound, splurting all of the food out into my face. It really felt like he did it on purpose to get at me. I carried on trying but he wouldn't take it and I felt more and more miserable. In the end I just gave up, and gave him a jar of ready-made stuff, and felt devastated.

This little interaction over food illustrates how difficult it can be for mothers and babies to deal with change and increased separation. Sean seems to be trying to process some rather mixed feelings about his mother. At first, he seemed to be teasing her a bit. There is something quite playful about his on-off response to her food, as he keeps her guessing about whether he'll deign to accept it or not, raising her hopes only to blow a raspberry at her. Perhaps he is experimenting with getting his angry feelings across.

Claire appears to be subdued and takes things very much to heart, possibly finding it hard to come to terms with losing the early closeness with her baby, when she was with him all the time. But as she responds so immediately by feeling hurt, Sean picks up that he has found a powerful tool with which to make an impact. It is striking how often babies – not to mention toddlers or adolescents – can find the exact button to press to get a reaction from their parents, negative as well as positive, and then keep pressing it, as if fascinated by their own power.

Just as a mother can feel devastated when a baby rejects her breast milk, Claire feels crushed when Sean refuses her food. Although she may not be aware of it at the time, she is probably deeply affected by returning to work. On some level she may be worried that Sean is angry with her, that she has inflicted too much suffering on him, that he will never forgive her. Because of this, it matters even more deeply to her that he should appreciate her food, which has become a sign that he still loves and wants her.

For Sean, as for all babies and young children, triumphing over his mother seems exciting at first, but it will also be very worrying, and at some stage the worries will surface. Later that afternoon as Claire changed his nappy, Sean became downcast and miserable. He hit himself in the face with a toy and cried very bitterly. Claire was able to comfort him and they were reconciled to one other. Not unusually, it was when Sean had hurt himself and obviously needed his mother's comfort that she could regain her confidence, certain once more that she was loved and wanted.

The impact of guilt

Perhaps Claire found it easier to see that her son was suffering and to comfort him when she could be completely sure that his pain wasn't due to anything she might have done to him. This time he'd definitely inflicted it on himself. It is very common that when we are feeling guilty – about returning to work, weaning from the breast, and so on – we are less able to see our babies for themselves, and are more likely to attribute anger or despair to them which might or might not actually be there. In these moments we can very easily feel "got at", and under the burden of our own guilt can find it hard to offer comfort as we would usually do, or to endure any criticisms or mild hostility without becoming persecuted. For underneath all of his anger and his teasing, Sean loves his mother as deeply as ever, and needs her to remember and hold fast to this knowledge, however much he might push at the limits.

Caught up in such situations, where there is a maelstrom of strong emotions, it is rarely possible to fathom out what might be going on there and then, let alone trying to put things right. When we are feeling robust and relatively sure of ourselves, a bit of hostility or rejection from our babies – or even a great deal of hostility or rejection – can be seen as part of our lot as parents, taken seriously but not too much to heart. The baby will see that we have taken her feelings on board, but are not too badly wounded: the boundaries are still intact.

But when we are feeling unsure of ourselves, guilty or depressed, rejection can take on a whole new meaning, and our baby suddenly assumes much more power over us. This can be worrying for both parties, and sometimes it takes a third person to help a parent to regather their adult perspective and defuse the situation. But this sort of interplay between angry and loving feelings is very much part of the deepening relationship. Some conflicts and misunderstandings are inevitable, especially at times of transition, when both baby and parents are struggling with the challenge of moving apart and moving on, surviving new separations and weathering the sadness and anger that surface on both sides.

Anxieties about childcare

Letting somebody else become a central figure in our baby's life, especially somebody outside of the family, can be more difficult than many parents expect. Much stress and agonizing usually accompany the choice of day-care that feels right for your baby, especially when she is still very young.

Joy describes how she left her eight-month-old baby with a nanny for one day a week.

> She was very good and experienced, but I worried all day about whether she would drop him, or let him have an accident. I couldn't bear for her to feed him, I didn't trust her to give him healthy food, so I used to prepare all his meals myself, even though it took ages and she kept saying she could do it herself. After a while I realized it just wasn't working. She was very experienced and a nice woman, but I never felt relaxed about leaving him in her hands. After a while I moved him to a nursery and everything seemed much easier.

Sometimes our guilty feelings about leaving our babies at all can be transferred onto worries about the person we are leaving them with. We can also feel reluctant to accept that the baby might benefit from forming a close relationship with somebody other than ourselves, even if they do things differently. Some mothers, like Joy, find it easier to leave their baby in a less intimate environment like a nursery, where possibly the underlying rivalries or ambivalence towards "substitute mothers" is less raw.

Mothers who are lucky enough to leave their babies with someone they feel close to – the baby's father, perhaps, or their own mother – can find themselves much calmer about leaving the baby, and letting her enjoy this other relationship. Whatever kind of childcare we choose, if we can genuinely feel that we have found a safe pair of hands, the baby will pick this up, and feel safer too – which means that separations should be less stressful for all concerned.

Letting the baby miss her mother

Some mothers find it difficult to acknowledge that their babies are becoming attached to their new carers, and enjoying the new opportunities that are opening up to them. Giving up our exclusive relationship with a baby is often painful and it is difficult to be generous with our baby's affections. But it is equally common that in our guilt and anxiety about leaving our babies, we overlook the fact that however happy they might be with childminders, nurseries or relatives, they will still be aware of our absence – it will matter to them. Sometimes a baby might show no signs of distress during the day, but suddenly seem more anxious at other separations, like bedtime, or, like Sean, suddenly refuse to eat her mother's food, around the time she returns to work. Another baby might greet her mother's return with apparent indifference, or even unhappiness, appearing to prefer staying with her childminder.

It is very easy to miss the connection between these events and the fact that our baby really is missing us, especially when we need to believe that she is completely happy with her new routine. The truth is, a baby is capable of having a lovely time with granny, or a childminder, or at nursery, while still missing her mother; her feelings about her mother's absences may show themselves in many different ways. Some babies can hold themselves together during periods of separation, perhaps keeping a lid on their upset feelings, making do with what is on offer, and this can last for a while even after their mother returns. It is expecting a lot for a baby to switch from one mode to another, greeting us with joyful embraces each time we decide to make a reappearance. And for most babies, the storm will break at some point, when they feel safe enough to show their mother how they feel deep down inside, whether this translates into falling into her arms for a cuddle, or kicking and screaming all the way home.

Of course there are times when a mother's return to work really does put her baby under too much strain. Perhaps she has gone back before the baby can manage without her, or for more hours than the baby can cope with. It is important that we remain open to what is really happening for our baby, monitoring carefully what she really can and can't manage – and, if we possibly can, to alter our plans if she needs us to. Obviously, some women face financial or contractual obligations which can be very rigid, leaving them with no choice but to continue with a situation that is far from ideal for themselves or their child. This is painful, and makes it both more difficult and more vital to remain in touch with the baby's feelings and help her through as sensitively as possible. For women who return to work knowing that they will have to negotiate a more gradual return, a reduction in hours or a change in childcare arrangements if their baby needs them to, the whole process is less intimidating.

During a return to work, and particularly in the weeks leading up to it, things are bound to feel more turbulent and there will be increased anxiety on both sides. Sometimes it takes some time before things settle back into place. But when the balance is right, women who are lucky enough to enjoy their work can discover that a bit of time away can make them appreciate and enjoy their babies even more.

Weaning from the breast

Many of the issues around returning to work are also relevant to weaning from the breast. But for many people, there is a particular poignancy around this separation.

Mothers often fear that they will lose their special place in their baby's affections after breastfeeding ends. Some dread causing distress by withdrawing such an important source of comfort, closeness and security. Breastfeeding is often seen as a special link with a baby's earliest life, representing her first experience of being held, fed, reassured and loved. In letting this go, it can seem as though the link with this precious part of the baby's life will be lost forever. On top of this, the experience of receiving comfort, closeness and love through breastfeeding is not only the baby's. The prospect of giving it up can feel like a major wrench for the mother in her own right.

Sometimes the decision to wean is made because of a return to work or other practicalities, but sometimes the decision has to be based on what feels right for the mother, and for the baby. When this is the case, our babies need us to be strong for them, letting them know sensitively but firmly when we feel that the time has come for breastfeeding to end. For if we are too wary of hurting our babies' feelings, we can lose sight of the fact that they also need our help in imposing limits on their needs and desires. They are not going to let us know when they've had enough and are ready to stop. If we are carrying on breastfeeding (or anything else) beyond what we really feel comfortable with, postponing the dreaded moment, we are not doing much good for ourselves or for our babies in the longer run. As we know, a baby can quickly feel too powerful, fearing that she can take as much as she likes from us, that we lack the strength to say "No". It will help her more if we can find the courage to keep to the boundaries we have set. This way we can help her to learn through experience how to deal with change and loss, backed by a mother who is strong enough to bear it with her.

At the other end of the scale, some mothers find themselves belittling the impact of weaning, possibly hardening themselves to their baby's feelings of loss, and to their own, perhaps by getting it over with quickly, preferring not to dwell on what weaning might mean to the baby, or to themselves. Such mothers may manage the situation in this way because it seems easier to deal with, and they might assume it will be easier for the baby too. On the surface, it can seem this way. But again, the baby is missing an important opportunity to get to know herself better. If she is helped to negotiate the pains and mixed feelings of this transition in a way that really means something to her, this will stand her in better stead for understanding and coping with loss or separation next time she encounters them.

The benefits of moving on

The end of breastfeeding can also be positive. Other members of the family might be relieved that the exclusivity between mother and baby is less pronounced: fathers and siblings, and grandparents too, can get more of a look-in. Mothers often feel relieved that their bodies are their own again, that they can claim back another part of their lives, and that the relationship is moving on to the next phase. Some mothers find that their babies actually seem to become more openly affectionate after weaning. One mother described how soon after weaning her one-year-old, he began to approach her spontaneously to give her a kiss – something he had never done while she was still breastfeeding him. Perhaps even the baby being weaned, if she is really ready to move on, has a sense of relief and pride herself, however much this is mixed with sadness.

Most mothers will cherish the memories of their babies at the breast for years after they have been weaned, and for long after the child herself has a conscious memory of being breastfed. Jo describes how the memories of breastfeeding remained strong, four years after weaning her baby.

I felt incredibly sad when I stopped breastfeeding her. In fact, I was probably more upset than she was, and it took me quite a while to get over it. But even now, she might be gulping her juice from a beaker, gazing at me with that particular look of concentration, or approaching a fork-full of food in a certain way, and I suddenly see the baby in her again, drinking away at the breast. It can bring a lump to my throat, suddenly seeing that baby again, who will never come back. But then, that baby has turned into this beautiful child, and I feel so proud of how far she's come.

It is important for children that parents hold on to memories of their infancy, seeing them both as they are now and as they used to be. This experience of being fully known and held in mind helps the child to feel integrated, secure and understood as she moves further away from her baby self. And just as somewhere in her mind she will always retain memories of the helplessness of her early infancy, albeit on an unconscious level, she will also retain a distant memory of the good experiences of babyhood, including the comfort and closeness of being held and fed at her mother's breast. During the pangs of weaning, it may be comforting to think that these half-memories will remain inside her, consolidating her knowledge of what it means to be loved and nourished, helping her to tackle whatever challenges life has in store.

In each of these transitions, returning to work or weaning from the breast, we tend to fear that our baby won't be able to endure the pain we are inflicting on her. But just as even the most miserable or furious baby can wake up and give us a beaming smile in the morning, there is usually a place for pride and elation in all situations where loss or separation have been successfully negotiated. Both mother and baby can find that we have come out the other end with something achieved: the love is still there, the anger, panic or sadness have been survived. Perhaps we and the baby are both stronger than we thought.

Conclusion

By the end of the first year we no longer have that tiny, warm and soft baby in our arms, who is almost an extension of our own body, who will fall asleep on our shoulder or mould his body into ours in such a tender, trusting way. The early phase of such closeness has given way to a more complex and deeper relationship. We are now faced with a little person who can be irresistibly sweet, bossy, tenacious, infuriating, and for whom we can feel overwhelming love, but who is not ours in the same way – someone who is setting out to become a toddler.

Yet while your one-year-old may seem a million miles away from the newborn baby – bombarded by helpless, panicky states or blissful content-ment – these more primitive, infantile feelings do not disappear entirely. They may occasionally surge up again in early childhood, only receding further as he leaves infancy far behind him. By the time he is an adult, he will very rarely meet these feelings in such a raw form again – perhaps not until he has a baby of his own.

Further Reading

Daws, D. (1989) *Through the Night: Helping Parents and Sleepless Infants*. London: Free Association Books.

Harris, M. (1975) *Thinking about Infants and Young Children*. Strath Tay, Perthshire: Clunie Press.

Phillips, A. (1999) *Saying "No": Why It's Important for You and Your Child*. London: Faber and Faber.

Winnicott, D.W. (1964) *The Child, the Family and the Outside World*. London: Penguin.

Helpful Organizations

Association for Post-Natal Illness (APNI)
145 Dawes Road
London SW6 7EB
Tel: 020 7386 0868
www.apni.org
Support for women with post-natal depression

Cry-sis
BM Cry-sis
London WC1N 3XX
Tel: 020 7404 5011 (7 days a week, 9 a.m. to 10 p.m.)
www.cry-sis.com
Helpline for families with excessively crying or sleepless babies

Gingerbread Association for One Parent Families
7 Sovereign Close
Sovereign Court
London E1W 2HW
Tel: 020 7488 9300
Advice line: 0800 018 4318
www.gingerbread.org.uk
Support for lone parent families

Home-Start
2 Salisbury Road
Leicester LE1 7QR
Tel: 0116 233 9955
www.home-start.org.uk
Practical and emotional support for parents in their own home

La Leche League
PO Box 29, West Bridgford
Nottingham NG2 7NP
Tel: 0845 120 2918
www.laleche.org.uk
Breastfeeding information and support helpline

Maternity Alliance
Third Floor West 2–6 Northburgh Street
London EC1V 0AY
Tel: 020 7490 7638
www.maternityalliance.org.uk
Information on maternity care and rights

National Childbirth Trust
Alexandra House, Oldham Terrace
Acton
London W3 6NH
Tel: 0870 444 8707 (enquiries) 0870 444 8708 (breastfeeding counselling)
www.nctpregnancyandbabycare.com
Information and support for mothers

Parentline Plus
24-hour helpline: 0808 800 2222
www.parentlineplus.org.uk
Information and support for parents

Parents Anonymous
Tel: 020 7233 9955 (7 p.m. to midnight)
www.parentsanonymous.org
Helpline for parents

Under-fives Counselling Service
The Tavistock Clinic
120 Belsize Lane
London NW3 5BA
Tel: 020 7435 7111
www.tavi-port.org (see Patient Services, Infant Mental Health Service)

Index